Journey of the Heart

"First book about deaconesses and home missioners authored by a deaconess from the USA! Deaconess Sharon McCart grounded and connected herself deeply in the situation, struggles, and hopes of the community. She witnessed how deaconesses and home missioners found joy and remained committed to serving God and his people—and how these heroes without capes continuously work for justice, love, and service. *Journey of the Heart* will surely inspire and challenge readers to face whatever battles lie ahead with courage and faith! This book invites us to walk together, connect deeply, and embrace the call to serve. Come, let's journey together!"

—**Sheila Faye Dayrit-Binuya**, Chairperson, Commission on Deaconess Service, Philippines Central Conference (2017–2025), The United Methodist Church

"*Journey of the Heart* is captivating, drawing readers into the courageous witness of deaconesses and home missioners in the Philippines. Through personal reflection, rich storytelling, and careful listening, McCart illuminates lives marked by solidarity with those in the margins, offering a moving portrait of vocation, justice, and the enduring spirit of the Order of Deaconess and Home Missioner."

—**Megan Hale**, Executive, Office of Deaconess and Home Missioner, United Women in Faith

"Dr. McCart's book is a must read for all who follow Jesus, the servant leader of the church. From this book the reader will learn from the faithful hearts of the deaconesses and home missioners of the Philippines the meaning of God's call to discipleship, the priority of ministry in the margins, the imperative of justice ministry, and the call to intentional solidarity with one another. Vital prayer and connection to God brings strength for this work as does the joy of worship and relationships. Dr. McCart explores questions about God's call to servant ministry and the sacrifices required for the sake of the Gospel."

—**Peggy Johnson**, United Methodist Bishop

"United Methodist deaconesses in the Philippines could aptly be called unsung heroines of the faith. But with her book, *Journey of the Heart*, Sharon Rae McCart has made sure that is no longer the case. With sheer grit and determination, fueled by a passion and love for deaconess/home missioners and the work that they do, McCart journeyed several times to the Philippines—notwithstanding martial law, Covid, and very rough terrains—to live amongst them, and to witness how they carried out their various ministries faithfully, and with great dedication. While she lifts up the exemplary witness and faith of these deaconess/home missioners, some of whom faced dangerous risks for standing up for justice, human rights, and on behalf of the poor and oppressed, Sharon Rae McCart's own faith shows through in the stories she told of them, and in her expressions of Christian mission as being in solidarity with 'the least of these' (Matt 25:40)."

—**Rebecca Asedillo**, Deaconess

Journey of the Heart

What I Have Learned from United Methodist Deaconess/Home Missioners in the Philippines

Sharon Rae Gollery McCart

RESOURCE *Publications* • Eugene, Oregon

JOURNEY OF THE HEART
What I Have Learned from United Methodist Deaconess/Home Missioners in the Philippines

Resource Publications
An Imprint of Wipf and Stock Publishers
199 W. 8th Ave., Suite 3
Eugene, OR 97401

www.wipfandstock.com

PAPERBACK ISBN: 979-8-3852-7339-3
HARDCOVER ISBN: 979-8-3852-7340-9
EBOOK ISBN: 979-8-3852-7341-6

VERSION NUMBER 03/30/26

In memory of Zara and Jurain, who were committed to serving their communities, and who were taken from those who needed them by extrajudicial killings.

To Deaconess Joy Prim, who started all of this by helping me buy a one-way ticket to Manila.

To my mom, Virginia Gollery, who never tried to talk me out of traveling even when she was worried that it was dangerous, and who listened to my long stories.

And to my husband, Dale, who has always encouraged me to do everything God calls me to do.

Contents

Preface

> "In the last days," God says, "I will pour out my Spirit on all people. Your sons and daughters will prophesy. Your young will see visions. Your elders will dream dreams." (Acts 2:17)

SMALL IN STATURE AND strong of spirit, retired Deaconess Doring (Doroteo) Bravo was an example of what courage is. I met her over a decade ago, when I served as the pastor of a church where nearly all the members were Filipino Americans. They were from three different regions of the Philippines, each with its own language and customs. It took me a long time to realize I wasn't trying to understand one other culture and maybe learn one new language. I was trying to learn three. It was an overwhelming challenge. I thought if I could visit the Philippines, I might have a chance of beginning to understand the members of the church so I could serve them better. I could not make that visit while I was at that church, but I had begun to dream about it because of Deaconess Doring.

By the time I met her, she was a naturalized US citizen in her late eighties. Her twelve children were grown with children and grandchildren of their own. She was a member—the matriarch—of the congregation. During World War II, the family told me after she passed, Deaconess Doring had carried out her ministry right next to the Japanese encampment, walking to where she would teach the children and serve the people under the eyes of the occupying troops with her Bible clutched to her chest. The Japanese soldiers saw her and called out, "Kristiyano! Kristiyano!" but they did not stop her. She continued visiting and serving the people despite the danger. No one else I have ever met has shown more courage than this story reveals.

Traveling to the Philippines would take a different kind of courage for me. Going so far out of my comfort zone, I needed to trust that God would keep me safe while I traveled. This was not something I did without hesitation. It would have been much easier to stay home, but the thought of this trip would not leave me. I heard God calling me there.

Although I had met Doring in 2009, I never saw a deaconess in action until 2014, when I attended United Methodist Women (now United Women in Faith, or UWF) Assembly[1] for the first time. I witnessed the consecration of about a dozen deaconess/home missioners. Until then, I had not known that deaconesses still existed and had never even heard the title "home missioner." After that service, I learned that the Order of Deaconess/Home Missioner was a lay (not ordained) order, a covenant community that prays for and supports each other and serves God by serving the community around them. I had left being a church pastor a couple of years before, realizing that congregational ministry was a poor fit for me. However, I was still in ministry, serving in Disability Ministries at both the denominational and regional (annual conference) levels. But those positions had term limits, and I had no support system outside of those two committees. I needed something to be part of permanently.

Discovering the Order of Deaconess/Home Missioner was like God opening a door for me. I soon began the application process and was consecrated at the 2018 Assembly. By then, I had been to the Philippines once and met about a dozen deaconesses there. I hadn't met many in the US because there weren't (and still aren't) many in the Western US, where I live. What I know about deaconesses, then, I have learned mostly in the Philippines. As I have spent

1. UWF Assembly is a meeting of mostly women and some men from all over the world. It takes place every four years and lasts three to four days. The agenda includes worship, celebration, and theology and social justice studies.

time with the deaconess/home missioners there, I have learned a lot that I want to share—the importance of their work in the United Methodist Church and beyond, their faithfulness, their hope and joy, as well as their dedication to serving God and humanity, and also how to overcome challenges, how to pray, how to find joy, and how to stay faithful to God during very difficult times.

Disclaimer

I am not Filipina; I am White. I am a deaconess in the US, not the Philippines. Even though the people I interviewed gave me many insights into their perspectives (gifts that I cherish), I write from my own viewpoint, my own experience. This is a limitation in interpreting the stories I have been privileged to hear, but I have done my best to listen well, to be respectful and careful as I write, knowing that I have been trusted with very precious thoughts and experiences.

Although I refer to my trips as "mission trips," I do not consider myself to be a missionary. Instead, I call myself a "reverse missionary." Instead of traveling to the Philippines to teach or preach, I have traveled to the Philippines to learn. My heart has been changed, and, as a result, I now see the world in a different way, influenced by the viewpoints and theologies of the people I have met. I am sharing what I learned with people in the US and hope they will be impacted by it.

What Is a Deaconess/Home Missioner?

The Book of Discipline of the United Methodist Church (our rule book) defines "deaconess/home missioners" in paragraph 1913 as follows:

> Deaconesses and home missioners function through diverse forms of service directed toward the world to make known in the fullness of his ministry and mission, which mandate that his followers:

a. Alleviate suffering;

b. Eradicate causes of injustice and all that robs life of dignity and worth;

c. Facilitate the development of full human potential; and

d. Share in building global community through the church universal.[2]

We are lay, not ordained. The *Discipline* adds that we are "professionally trained persons who have been led by the Holy Spirit to devote [our] lives to Christlike service under the authority of the Church," held accountable by United Women in Faith (formerly United Methodist Women), consecrated by a bishop to a lifetime of love, justice, and service, and commissioned by a local bishop to our appointments, which can be to any setting approved by the United Women in Faith.[3]

2. The United Methodist Church, *Book of Discipline*, para. 1913.

3. The United Methodist Church, *Book of Discipline*, para. 1913.

Acknowledgments

THIS BOOK WAS DEACONESS Emma A. Cantor's idea. She invited me into her world and shared her heart's vision, which helped my own heart to grow large enough to hold both the pain and the joy that I encountered in the Philippines. I am very grateful to Emma for this, but, even more, for her love, support, and friendship. I will always remember our times together, and I pray that someday she and I will sit on a beautiful beach and reminisce together.

Much gratitude also goes to the staff at the Board of Women's Work in the United Methodist Philippines Regional Conference for making my research possible. In particular, I thank Jennifer Ferariza Meneses for planning my itineraries, Deaconess Bless De Leon for being my host and guide extraordinaire, and Hannah Cantor for coordinating arrangements. You are all God's gifts to me.

I thank the staff at the National Council of Churches Philippines (NCCP) for teaching me the culture, history, and sociopolitical context. Without them, I would not understand what solidarity and resistance mean, and this book would not exist, because I never would have asked the questions that drove me to write it.

I am especially grateful to Rev. Cheryl Borbe for hearing God's call to disability ministries at the first disability consultation and forming a powerful disability ministries team. A special thanks also to Pow Cantiller, who keeps me updated on the wonderful work they and the rest of the team are doing, and to Arnel Oroceo, who accomplished so much as part of that team. Arnel passed into the arms of Christ on January 1, 2026, a great loss to so many of us.

Above all, I thank the deaconess/home missioners of the Philippines for sharing their time with me, whether I interviewed them or not, whether I have written about them or not. To all of them I say, "You are my *kasamas*, my sisters and brothers, my coworkers, all of you. *Maraming, maraming salamat*!" Here is a list of the interviewees, all deaconess/home missioners except as noted, in the order of interviews:

Emma A. Cantor, Norma Dollaga, Mimi Lopez, Michelle Dudang-Ortiz, Helen Asuncion, Jessica Cecilio, Karen Salibio, Olga Ducut, Coleen Capuno (now Rev.), Lady Lhou Ganal, Ruth Trube, Janisa Bole-Galeos, Christine DeGuzman-Cortado, Michelle Salado, Joel Gacote, Romelito Gallardo, Esther Valdez-Aquino, Jovelyn Unagap-Lopez, Adeline Cornito, Hazel Sablay, Julievee Tapiu, Gemma Labagan, April Grace Martinez, Darlene Marquez-Caramanzana, Phebe Crismo, Aliah Dizon, Chita Framo, and Zarla Raguindin (currently inactive). All of you were so generous with your time and your experiences. I could not have written this book without every one of you. A special thank-you to Elijah Alivia-Layugan for being the mother of my adorable godson.

I would also like to thank my brother, Martin R. Gollery, who offered his advice as a professional photographer to improve my photo choices.

I am also indebted to Dr. Shan Overton, whose brilliance and persistence created the DMin program in Creative Writing and Public Theology at Pittsburgh Theological Seminary, and to Dr. Donna Giver-Johnston, her successor as director of the program, who helped me to finish well. I am also grateful to Liberty Ferda for being the reader for this book, and to Hunter Farrell for being the reader of my theology paper, both of whom made this book much better. I also thank the incredible members of my cohort, who taught me that I *am* a writer!

1

Solidarity Missions

Manila and Mindanao, 2017

In 2017, five years after I left being a church pastor, Joy Prim, a friend of mine (who would be consecrated as a deaconess in 2022), was organizing one of a series of annual Solidarity Mission Trips to the Philippines. Hosted by the National Council of Churches Philippines (NCCP), the focus would be on learning about the socioeconomic and political situations. In addition, relationships would begin that would lead to solidarity and partnerships. In previous years I had wanted to join the team, but my schedule did not allow it. Finally, my calendar was clear. I contacted Joy. I had many questions. She answered them all. I decided to go. More questions came up, especially when the news broke that Mindanao, the southernmost island of the Philippines, where we were going, had just been put under martial law. She assured me we would be safe, and if Mindanao became unsafe, we would go north of Manila to Central Luzon instead. Only when it was nearly time to go did I learn the team would be just the two of us. The rest had backed out. I trusted Joy and I was very excited to go. My stomach clenched and my breathing was quick. It felt a lot like being nervous, except that I couldn't wait to get on the plane. For me, excitement and nervousness are separated by only a razor's edge. Excitement fuels courage, while nervousness is formed of fear. I had to keep my emotions focused in the right direction. I had to remember Deaconess Doring serving under the watchful eye of the Japanese troops and find my own bravery.

Visiting Prisoners

The first item on our itinerary was a visit to women political prisoners.[1] We took food because rations for prisoners were very minimal, consisting of only two meals of thin broth each day. We waited under a large overhang for the women to come down from their fourth-floor cell. They were in a men's prison because the women's prison was full. This prison was full, too, with two or three people per bed.

The building was U-shaped, with a courtyard in the middle. The cells were open to the weather on the sides toward the courtyard, so prisoners could see each other. I saw a man signing to someone on the other side. Whether he was deaf or not, sign language was a good way to communicate in that place, filled with the rise and fall of many people talking and occasionally shouting. Then I saw a man come to the bars of his cell on the second floor dressed in what appeared to be biblical robes, an outfit made even more striking by the rule that prisoners must wear a yellow T-shirt. I could not help thinking I was seeing the apostle Paul, who was, after all, a prisoner for God in Rome. The mental image I had of Paul being in a comfortable prison cell evaporated in a blink.

We waited a long time for the women to come down. One of them was being held back by the guard. She was a new prisoner and her name was not on the list of people we were visiting. The rest would not come down without her. Our NCCP host told the guard that we would not leave without seeing the women. As we waited for this standoff to end, a typhoon moved in. The wind

1. *Rappler* (an online Philippine newspaper) and Karapatan (a human rights watch organization) are good sources for more information about political prisoners. One helpful article can be found at National Council of Churches in the Philippines, "Talk About Political Prisoners."

picked up and the warm rain poured down. I was grateful to be under cover.

Finally, the women came down. They were young to middle-aged. Some had been imprisoned for years and others had arrived more recently. We began our visit seated in a large oval, spread out a bit, but as we spoke, we moved closer to the back wall to stay drier as the rain blew in harder, and closer to each other to hear as the rain pounded harder on the metal roof.

As the women told their stories of being arrested, many taken at night from their children, I struggled to keep my composure. My heart was breaking for them. They had been arrested as suspects in murders, attempted murders, having illegal explosives or other weapons, and other false charges. In one case, the murder victim had turned up alive, yet the accused woman was still in prison. Another woman and her husband had been arrested at the same time for having explosives under the bed they slept in with their four children. One woman had been arrested as she pushed her baby in a stroller. The police claimed they had found explosives tucked in next to the baby. Any skepticism I felt fell away as I realized that no sane mother would put her babies in danger, and these women seemed very sane. This was where I began to understand solidarity as believing what people are saying even when it's difficult to listen. I only asked questions for clarification and additional information.

My questions were patiently and soberly answered, except one. When I asked if they knew when they would be released, they laughed. Some of them had not even been formally charged. The length of their sentences depended on the persistence of their lawyers or advocates. Meanwhile, two meals of thin gruel a day meant the women were emaciated and always hungry. Still, they did not eat the food we brought until after we left, planning, perhaps, to share with others. We knew that food would make a big difference for that day. I wished it were possible to visit and bring food every day.

By the time our visit was over, the typhoon was flooding many streets. Our trip back across Metro Manila was slow and cautious as night fell and the typhoon did not abate. This gave me time to process and to ask Joy and our host questions. I cannot remember what I had expected this trip to be like, but I was not ready for this. This prison visit was the part of the trip I had been the most anxious about. What I didn't know at the time was that it was not the only part that would be difficult emotionally.

Extrajudicial Killings

Back in the NCCP building, I was sickened to hear about extrajudicial killings being committed as part of the "war on drugs."[2] In neighborhoods where drug trafficking is suspected, men are shot at night by masked motorcycle riders riding in tandem. No investigation is ever done, no suspects ever brought to justice. Mothers and wives and children of the men are left to grieve without any hope of justice. We learned all of this and more from Deaconesses Norma Dollaga and Rubylin Litao, who were among the first deaconesses I met. They are the founders of an NCCP-related organization called Rise Up for Life and for Rights. Rise Up supports women as they grieve and teaches women how to support each other as they pursue justice. I will write more about Rise Up in a later chapter.

I also learned about the Philippine Ecumenical Peace Platform from Ofelia Cantor. There is a civil war in the Philippines between the government of the Republic of the Philippines and the National Democratic Front of the Philippines. It is crucial to work for a just and lasting peace when human rights are violated with impunity, and where indigenous peoples and the poor are denied the assistance they need. Peace talks had been taking place in Norway, and progress had been made until President Rodrigo Duterte suspended the talks shortly after taking office in 2016. Work to

2. This information is supported by Human Rights Watch, "Philippines Events of 2023," as well as reports made to the World Council of Churches, arbitrary executions, detention in Philippines focus of statements at World Council of Churches, "WCC Statement," and others.

restart the talks continues while this book is being written in 2025. Progress continues to be slow.[3]

In Mindanao Under Martial Law

Joy and I traveled to Mindanao to spend five days in a school for Lumad (indigenous) children and youth. Built with funding from church people, the school was its own community, with students and staff living on campus.

The computer room, library, and elementary classrooms.

There was a health clinic on campus because it was a long trip to the nearest hospital. It served not only the school, but the wider community. The students ranged from preschool through college age. Our time at this school has left indelible marks on my heart. As a teacher, I was impressed by the breadth of the curriculum, which covered not only the government requirements but also respected the heritage of the students with courses in topics such

3. Read more about the peace talks at the url in the Bibliography for: National Council of Churches in the Philippines, "Church Leaders."

as preparing herbal medicines (I was given one of the medicines to use because I had a cough and by the time I left I was no longer coughing) and their traditional way of organic farming. We were fortunate to be there on one of their quarterly cultural nights. These nights wrapped up the topic they had been focused on, and this quarter they had studied healthy habits. I mostly understood the skits despite not understanding the language, laughing at many and being moved by others. In addition, there were tribal songs and dances. Some of the dances included lit torches and athletic moves that made me hold my breath.

The students were from a dozen or more tribes, each with a different language. Most of their parents were illiterate and could not read the documents that allowed the government to sell their ancestral lands to foreign corporations. This was why education was so important to them.

Traditional indigenous farming on the side of a hill.

They needed to be able to read documents for themselves before they signed them. It was important enough to move away from family, important enough to do whatever it took to have a school, important enough for faculty and staff to take risks, and important enough for churches and other supporters to raise the funds. Seeing so many people willing to give up so much challenged me. I would soon go back to my comfortable, privileged life in the United States. These people would continue to live under martial law, with only the very basics available. There were no hot water or washing machines or fully stocked supermarkets. Cars are out of most people's financial reach. My heart opened as my mind absorbed what it was like to live at that school. On our final night there, I tried to sleep on the same thin pad on the concrete floor of a preschool classroom where I had slept every night and wondered how people could choose that life. While there was no possibility for them to choose the kind of comfortable life that I am used to, the students could have stayed with their parents and the faculty could have been working at a school in town. Instead, they were together in this little valley surrounded by banana plantations owned by giant foreign corporations, staying even when the president had given the OK to the military to bomb the school for being a training school for child soldiers. The adults continued teaching the children because education is important enough to take risks. The children stayed because they believed education would give them a better future. There, in the early morning in that classroom, with a carabao[4] chewing grass outside my window, it occurred to me that resistance to government policies and decrees is more than writing letters to your representatives or signing petitions, more than marching in the streets, even more than getting arrested for civil disobedience. Resistance is building a school hidden away in the hills and educating people the government does not want educated. Resistance is doing what is right even when the world around you tells you not to. Resistance is taking concrete action.

That night, my solidarity was stretching. I cared deeply about these people in this place that I had never had a flickering

4. A type of water buffalo used like an ox to help with farming.

thought about before, a concern about problems I previously didn't know existed, and a desire to do what I could to help them find solutions to those problems.

Back to Metro Manila

As we returned to the Manila area, I felt exhausted by all I had seen and heard. As we were packing to return to the US, I told Joy that it had been an amazing trip, but I didn't think I would return. I felt my heart might tear to shreds if I came back. And then a funny thing happened.

Near the beginning of the trip, we had met Jennifer Ferariza Meneses serendipitously in the hallway of the NCCP office building. Jenn is the executive secretary of the United Methodist Board of Women's Work in the Philippines. She had another appointment to get to that day, but she wanted to talk to us and include other women leaders in the conversation. The only opening we could find on our itinerary was the last day of our trip, just before we headed to the airport. So, on that last day we met with Jenn, joined by Rev. Marie Sol Villalon and Liza Cortez, at a nearby restaurant for brunch to share about our ministries. Pastor Sol was (and still is) working for the Board of Church and Society with a focus on helping trafficked and exploited overseas workers. Liza, now retired, was the director of the Asuncion A. Perez Memorial Center, an agency that helps women and children in need. Jenn shared about her work, and I shared about the Disability Ministries Committee of The United Methodist Church, where I was serving as chair.

After we all finished sharing, the three women began to talk to each other in Tagalog. I ate my fern and salt egg salad in silence, the crispness of the young fern shoots and other greens contrasting perfectly with the salty softness of the brined hard-boiled eggs. I did not understand what they were saying. I was lost in thought, beginning to process my experiences. Then Pastor Sol said, "Sharon, we are just discussing what board the Disability Ministries Committee should go under!" I was so surprised my mouth fell open, then shut again as I tried to swallow. I looked at Joy. She was trying to hold back a chuckle. She had been listening to them. After a short exchange about which board would be the best fit, they went back to talking and I went back to eating and pondering. Then I heard my name again. I looked across at Jenn, who said, "Now we are beginning to plan the first national disability consultation for next year!" Joy laughed out loud while I sat silent, more than a bit stunned. A long moment passed before I looked at Joy and said, "I guess this means I'm coming back."

And I did.

Metro Manila in 2018

There had been one catch. I was asked to fundraise for the consultation, but I didn't understand that I was being asked to raise the entire budget. I was able to get a few pledges, but not enough to hold the event, so the consultation did not happen in 2018. I still went back because I had convinced my sister to go, with the goal of having this experience together. Joy recruited three students and a coleader, so that year we were a larger team of seven.

We again visited political prisoners, this time a group of men. Their stories were similar to those of the women we had met the year before about being arrested on false charges despite having solid alibis. When they had received their legal documents after a long wait, two of the men found that they were both charged with committing a crime together even though they had never met until they shared a prison cell. The anger and shock I felt over the injustices we had heard about on the first trip came back all over again. Even as I write this several years later, I am shaking my head in disbelief.

We heard again from justice workers about their challenging and important work, and we visited a museum in Intramuros, the old part of Manila, to learn the history of the Spanish colonial period, as well as a museum that chronicled the history of martial law under Ferdinand Marcos in the 1970s. But when it came time to go north to visit an indigenous community, the team left without me. I had injured my back a few months before and could not possibly hike up into the rugged Cordillera mountains. I stayed in Metro Manila. NCCP staff took me to meet previous political prisoners, to a press conference of people who had been arrested and beaten for being on strike (even though the strike was legal), and to a training session with an organization called Gabriela, where returned overseas workers who had been cheated and abused learned how to pursue charges against the agencies that had sent them to unsafe placements.[5]

I also visited a children's center, where I saw some of the same students I had met in Mindanao the year before. They had gone on *bakwit* (i.e., they had been evacuated) when the military took over their school because they didn't feel safe there anymore. I was glad to see them, but devastated for the reason. Asking them about the faculty, staff, and other students did not seem wise or kind. I only asked them about the future. I saw them again a few days later at a church service where one of the young men, Jurain, spoke. The year before he had been an upperclassman, one of the students.

5. It is difficult to find work that pays well enough to send children to school, access medical care, have a safe and secure home, etc., so at least 10 percent of the population become Overseas Foreign Workers (OFWs) and send money home to help their families. Although agencies make the placements, they do not always avoid placing workers in unsafe or abusive situations. Deaconess Joy Prim, who is now a missionary working with OFWs in Hong Kong, reports that some of them sleep on bathroom floors, in closets, or on living room couches, with no private bedrooms of their own. Rev. Sol Villalon, who works to repatriate abused OFWs, tells me that there are employers who lock the workers up on their days off, confiscate their phones, and/or refuse to pay them. I once met an OFW who was on her way home from Hong Kong for her mother's funeral. She had only been given three days for the trip, two of them spent traveling. Her employer refused to pay her before she left to ensure she would return.

Jurain speaking during a church service.

Then the students sang and we had lunch together. I am grateful that I saw them again. In 2022, Jurain, along with Chad, a health-care worker, and their drivers, were victims of an extrajudicial killing, their blood staining the soil of the banana plantations. They had returned to Mindanao, searching for students.[6] Jurain has a permanent home in my heart, and the memory of this unjust act will continue to spur me on to further acts of solidarity and resistance on behalf of all who are oppressed and marginalized. I continue to pray that the rest of the students have found their way back to their families or to some other safe place.

Solidarity Mission 2019, Negros

On this third trip, we joined a delegation from the World Council of Churches (WCC) on a Peace with Justice Pilgrimage. This time,

6. For more details, refer to the bibliography for: Butler, "Mindanao."

our time in the community would only be two days. Once again, my sister joined Joy and I on the trip, and a member of the WCC delegation went with us to the island of Negros, south of Manila, while other teams of delegates visited two other places. Our task was to find the facts in an extrajudicial killing case. We met with wives and daughters of victims. This is what we learned:

When a foreign corporation bought many acres of land to grow sugar cane, a highly profitable crop, many small farmers were displaced, including a group who are now known as the Sagay Nine. This meant they had lost the right to farm on their ancestral land, leaving them with nowhere to grow food for their families. Their children were starving. When they found a small patch of unused land on the sugar plantation, they petitioned several times for the right to use it. They were denied each time. Finally, in desperation, they spent all of one day planting that plot of land. After sunset, two of the men went to get something for everybody to eat. The rest settled in for the night. While the two were gone, they heard gunshots. When they returned to their friends, they found them shot dead. They were later framed for the murders. The lawyer who took up their case was later murdered on the porch of his office. His wife, also a lawyer, received death threats, as did the widows and grown children of the farmers.

When we were there, Negros was under a "declared State of lawlessness."[7] Every precaution was taken to keep us safe. The "fastest driver" on the island was hired to outrun any vehicle that followed as we traveled over the mountains to the other side of the island. We stayed only two nights, in different locations, behind locked and guarded gates. The danger was real, but I wasn't thinking about myself as much as I was feeling the pain of the families of the victims.

Back in Metro Manila, we gathered with the entire group to write a report. The process was stringent and comprehensive. It was

7. A declared state of lawlessness means that the president as commander-in-chief "may call out such armed forces to prevent or suppress lawless violence, invasion or rebellion" if necessary. See bibliography for Daguno-Bersamina, "Palace Explains 'State of Lawlessness.'"

later released by the World Council of Churches, adding this report to those written by the United Nations and other entities.[8] The Human Rights Council of the World Council of Churches passed a resolution decrying the human rights violations in the Philippines. I started a list of questions that I wanted to ask deaconess/home missioners, but the pandemic postponed all of that.

8. A later report by the WCC can be found in the bibliography under World Council of Churches, "Statement."

Interlude

Geographic and Economic Context

The country of the Philippines is an archipelago of over 7,500 islands in Southeastern Asia. With the northern tip about 750 miles (1,200 km) south of Taiwan and the southern end about 900 miles (1440 km) north of the equator, it spans about 900 miles, dividing the China Sea from the Pacific. This strategic political/military/economic position resulted in several hundred years of colonization by Spain, followed by over four decades by the US, and a three-year occupation by the Japanese military during the Second World War. After the war, the Philippines worked to be an independent nation, fighting against the belief of the US leaders that they were incapable of governing themselves.

The Philippines has a very high level of poverty, with many living in extreme poverty. The need to provide a better life for themselves and their families has resulted in a significant portion of the population migrating overseas to find better-paying employment. Unfortunately, some of the migrants become victims of wage theft, physical abuse, or human trafficking in other countries, including the US.

The country is very rich in natural resources. Unfortunately, this attracts foreign corporations but does not enrich the populace. Still, the beauty of the country, with its broad agricultural fields, the mountains formed and shaped by both ancient and current volcanic and seismic activity, and the abundant flowers and birds looks like paradise to many.

But both tropical heat and extreme poverty are oppressive. Frequent typhoons, flooding, severe earthquakes, and mudslides make life hazardous. Still, the hearts of the people pulse with love and hope.

2

Catching Emma Cantor's Vision

After three Solidarity Mission Trips, I had learned how beautiful the Philippines are, how warm and welcoming the people are, how hot and humid the weather is, and a great deal about the sociopolitical situation. The poor are extremely poor. Human rights violations and other injustices are egregious. The indigenous peoples are losing their ancestral lands. My heart could not take any more. I became depressed. I considered not returning as a measure of self-care.

But I could not avoid the truth that my spirit had found a home there. I longed to come back. I loved the country and the people. I wanted to know the deaconesses I had met better, and I wanted to meet the rest. I wanted to know how they serve, how they minister to people in the face of such overwhelming need, how they keep going in the face of such challenges. Deeper than that, I felt that Jesus was very close to me when I was there. I believe with all my heart that I was called to continue traveling to the Philippines.

But how could I come back? Could I somehow organize my own trip if I stepped out on my own, without being part of a team? During the pandemic, my team leader, Joy Prim, had been commissioned as a missionary to Hong Kong, and I did not feel qualified to lead a team. I didn't want to think that my travels to the

Philippines were over. While I may have, for a time, lacked sufficient confidence to travel on my own, I did not lack determination. That carried me through, with the help of Emma.

Deaconess Emma A. Cantor had hosted me at the end of my second visit, taking me to visit Harris Memorial College (one of the two deaconess training schools). We often communicated on social media. She had stayed at my sister's house when she visited the United States, and I had spent time with her there. We had become friends. So, I video-chatted with her one evening to talk about a way for me to return, a path to meeting more deaconesses and finding answers to my questions. Emma was serving as the United Women in Faith (UWF)[1] regional missionary in Southeast Asia, traveling to seven countries in addition to her homeland, the Philippines. I hoped that she could help me find a purpose and a plan for my next trip, because, as she told me, "The heart never stops envisioning," and mine was envisioning more trips to the Philippines.

Throughout the pandemic I had added to my list of questions. I found life difficult during the isolation and restrictions that were designed to keep us safe from COVID, and I wondered how the people of the Philippines were managing. I knew there were food shortages and financial difficulties and I could not imagine how deaconesses were managing to continue serving the people. I wanted to ask them, "How do you continue to serve when the needs are overwhelming? Where do you find joy when life is so hard? Who do you turn to when you face difficult challenges?"

These were only three of the questions I wanted to ask the deaconesses. I had felt discouraged many times, at a loss as to how to make any difference in a world which too often seems deficient in love and justice. How can I serve the needs I see everywhere but seem more sharply focused for me in the Philippines? How could I make even a very small difference in the suffering and oppression that exist everywhere? I didn't even know how to try. Is my confession of solidarity real when I can always go back to the United States, where I have more than enough of

1. Formerly United Methodist Women.

everything, when so many people don't have the barest necessities in the Philippines? How am I being called to serve and why? I believed I could find the answers to these questions in the Philippines, where deaconess/home missioners find ways to press on with strength and courage. Where they find ways to laugh and be joyful and love whole-heartedly, despite the suffering around them and the struggles they face personally. My heart longed for answers. I had to continue my visits to the Philippines and spend more time with deaconess/home missioners.

Emma had a vision long before I first traveled to the Philippines for a book that would document the work of deaconesses, so when I asked her for a plan to continue visiting, she had an answer ready. By the end of the conversation, she had convinced me I was the one to write this book. She believes it will strengthen the Order of Deaconess/Home Missioner, which in turn will strengthen the ecumenical, worldwide church. United Methodist deaconess/home missioners are part of the worldwide Diakonia, an organization which includes deaconesses, home missioners, deacons, and others in recognized lay and ordained ministries in many denominations. Imagine what the world might be like if more people were consecrated to serving others!

As I caught Emma's vision, it occurred to me that my vision can be shared with others, gaining strength and reach. My vision includes building relationships and raising awareness of the work so many are doing to grow the kin-dom of God, and it's not limited to this book. As I continue my work to build a bridge across the Pacific, I believe that I am doing my part to build God's kin-dom here on earth.

Emma, who retired while this book was in process, was an active deaconess for over four decades, appointed to a progression of positions, all serving women and children, including both the Women's Desk at the National Council of Churches Philippines and the Board of Women's Work in the Philippines Central Conference of The United Methodist Church. As the United Women in Faith regional missionary to Asia, she continued to use her expertise to teach other women about relationship-building and community organizing, empowering others to make their own communities stronger and healthier. She has lived out the love of Christ for all people by sharing her own heart with the world.

Born and raised in the Philippines, she does not fit the old stereotype of "missionary." Instead of exhorting people to convert to Christianity, her work empowered women and served children, improving their lives and strengthening the communities she visits. Her eyes are kind, and her smile is genuine.

Deaconess Emma A. Cantor

She laughs as easily as she smiles. Her voice is soft, never rising very much. I have heard her speak intensely and sometimes sadly, but never in anger, and never without hope and compassion. She resists talking about her accomplishments and hesitates to express how important her work is. She, with her humble heart, doesn't always seem to realize how bold her vision is, how much she is already changing the world, and how contagious her ideas are. Maybe I see the possibilities even more clearly than she does. I hope this book can help others see the impact deaconess/home missioners are having in many places. With additional deaconesses/home missioners, and a broadening of support, the world would become much closer to being the way God created it to be. To me, this is the purpose of everything we do. I think Emma sees that, too, and just finds it easier to show it than to say it.

As the United Women in Faith's regional missionary with women, children, and youth, Emma was assigned to the East Asia/Pacific region for gender training and leadership development. She found much joy in this work. She does not know the languages of all the places where she served, so she spoke through interpreters. Even at that, she feels "one has to see the heart in order to translate what they are saying." God has given her the gift of seeing the hearts of others, and, as a result, her heart that "does not stop envisioning" knew what was needed by the women she worked with. But while her heart empowers her to be in ministry, it also presents her with her biggest challenge. It is difficult for her to see so much need, especially among children, believing that there is very little she can do to change their situations. I suspect that she made more of a difference than she will ever know through her leadership training and community organizing and the spiritual and self-care practices that she teaches, all to help women become able to improve their lives and the circumstances of their families and communities.

Emma, like other deaconesses, is disciplined and hardworking. She is described by friends as being unshakeable, a true friend. She was well suited and well prepared for her missionary work, which took her to many places in South Asia, including Nepal, Indonesia, India, Myanmar, Cambodia, Sri Lanka, and many, many places in the Philippines.

Several of these countries have experienced war. Glory Dharmaraj, a UWF staff member, praised Emma's ways of tending to the spiritual needs of women. She worked with Emma many times. On one trip the two of them teamed up to address the trauma that widows of war in Nepal have felt. Glory told me they had each widow light a candle. I imagine the scene like this—each woman lit a candle and placed it in front of her. The flickering lights in the darkened room helped them focus, blocking out distractions. The women were instructed to talk to their husbands. Quickly the room became noisy as emotions—grief, anger, pain—poured out. Emma has a gift for developing methods like this that help women heal.

In addition to healing practices, Emma built relationships that nurtured growth, calmness, and wholeness of spirit. She drew out leadership skills and trained women to come together to better the circumstances of the community. Emma believes that "leadership capacity building is very, very important," and she knows that, in all countries, women are the most disadvantaged, the poorest of people. Her approach, then, was to train the women so well that the work continued to function without problems between her visits. She created space for others to become leaders. This is a new definition of "missionary," this focus on empowering and training people, building relationships, and meeting needs, collaborating and raising each other up. Emma had every qualification needed. Her wisdom and her love for people made her perfect for this work.

Even in areas where Christians are in the minority, she brought the light of Christ, and showed, in her tender, caring way, who Christ is and how God loves, to Christians and non-Christians alike. With her as my role model, I have learned to be gentle instead of angry, to invite transformation instead of insisting on change, to listen more than I speak, to see the ways culture impacts the ways faith is lived out. I have learned to develop the heart of Christ, the heart that never stops envisioning.

A million thanks—*maraming salamat*!—Emma, for opening the door of my heart so I could join you on this journey. I owe you more than I can say.

3

Transition

> Because you've made the Lord my refuge, the Most High, your place of residence—no evil will happen to you; no disease will come close to your tent. Because he will order his messengers to help you, to protect you wherever you go. (Ps 91:9–11)

Lockdown in Manila— A Pandemic Delay

On March 17, 2020, wearing the only mask I had, I stood in line to check my luggage at the Manila airport. The line was long. It had started forming at least two hours before the counter even opened. As the line crawled forward, I could see the board with the outgoing flights listed. As I watched, the status of at least six flights flipped to "Canceled." After the sixth one switched, the masked woman in front of me turned and said, "I hope ours isn't canceled." It was exactly what I was thinking.

I had arrived in Manila on March 10 to begin my project to document the work of deaconesses in the Philippines. It was my fourth trip to the Philippines. I had learned that the work of deaconesses in the Philippines is very important to the church and to the country as a whole. It deserves to be better known. I was there to begin interviewing deaconesses for this book.

Before I left California, I knew the pandemic was coming, but I didn't think it would come so quickly. I had purchased my plane ticket well in advance. It was only going to be a two-week trip. I thought the virus would hold off until I was back in the States. I was wrong.

When I got off the plane in Manila, I heard the word "lockdown" for the first time. My anxiety rose a bit, but I didn't know what it really meant yet. When I arrived at Decker Home for Retired Deaconesses, my "home away from home," in Quezon City, plans were undecided. My host, Deaconess Marlonie De Guzman Policarpio, told me that Metro Manila (which includes Quezon City) would be locked down in seventy-two hours. No one would be allowed to move around within the city or leave or enter it. Soldiers and police officers would enforce this mandate.

Marlonie had a presentation planned for an Annual Conference session, a regional meeting to conduct the business of The United Methodist Church, which started the day after I arrived and lasted two or three days. We could attend if we took a very early bus north the next morning, less than twelve hours after I arrived. I am trying to remember how long the trip took. I think it was eight hours, but it could have been ten, or maybe even twelve. Jet lag has blurred the memory, although I did not sleep. The bus was crowded with people going back to the province (their hometowns) before the lockdown began. We passed through expansive farmlands where I saw, among other things, awe-inspiring flocks of white herons rising up into the clear sky from the rice fields. We stopped often in cities, towns, and on the shoulder of the road to let people off, and a few people got on. Sometimes vendors stepped on board, selling local fruits and vegetables. Marlonie bought a kind of fruit I did not recognize from one of the vendors, a young man who claimed it would "cure your COVID"! It looked kind of like a thin cucumber, peeled like a banana, and was crunchy and sweet like an apple. Of course, he was trying to make money off a serious threat, but it was delicious, even if not medicinal. Or maybe it was! After all, I did not get COVID.

After a night's sleep, which alleviated my time-zone-enhanced fatigue only a little, we went to the church where the meeting was being held. Marlonie made her presentation successfully, and I interviewed eight deaconesses two at a time, keeping it short because the deaconesses were supposed to be in the plenary session. Unfortunately, the recording was lost. I have some scant notes and a few memories which, when combined, tell me that, among the eight deaconesses, there was diversity in their ages and years of experience. Their personalities varied from very outgoing to slightly shy. Some had taken leaves of absence while raising their children. Others remarked that they had to neglect their own children when they were needed by the church. None of them were still in the church they had been appointed to when they first began in ministry, and most had been moved by the bishop multiple times. I heard from them that some deaconesses have experienced sexism and/or some other kind of gender-related harassment. They were, naturally, very reluctant to speak about this in detail. I had the impression that these incidents often led to them being moved to another church. I later heard similar stories from other deaconesses in other places who told me that this was one of their most difficult challenges. But these dedicated women have found ways to continue serving God despite these incidents, still honoring their consecrations to a lifetime of love, justice, and service, still strong deaconesses.

On the positive side, all of them glowed when talking about children and youth. They all became deaconesses because they love children and want to teach them about God. This has been unanimous among everyone I interviewed, and seemingly universal among all deaconess/home missioners in the Philippines. Their love of children added to their love of God is the reason they joined the order.

On that trip I not only learned about these eight women; I learned that in the Philippines, deaconess/home missioners make reports at their annual conference sessions. Whether they could go on or come back from leave of absence had to be voted on by the body, among other things. This is very different from the US. I had never heard of a Deaconess/Home Missioner Report to Annual Conference. That's why I didn't know there were deaconesses in the US! So, despite recording problems and the impending COVID lockdown, I had begun learning more about the differences between the US and the Philippines within the Order of Deaconess/Home Missioner. I also learned how important the members of this lay order are to the churches in the area. They teach not only on Sunday mornings but also at the church-run schools during the week. They serve in every way they are needed in the church, including directing the choir, playing the organ or piano, organizing events, visiting the sick, etc. They are the strength of the churches.

As soon as the business of the conference ended for the day, we got on an overnight bus back to Manila. Although I slept on the bus, I went to bed when we got back to Decker. When I woke up, I found that Marlonie was gone, heading back to the province we had just visited, taking her family with her. My host, Wenelyn, granddaughter of Emma Cantor, asked me if I minded if she left, too. I did mind, because the fear I saw in her eyes made me afraid as well, but I denied it. She left quickly. I was not left alone at Decker. The cook and her young son were still there, along with my friend Rebecca Lawson and a few other residents.

My return flight was scheduled for March 23, but I had to leave sooner. Manila had been locked down as of March 15, and on the evening of March 16, the president had declared that the Manila airport would be shut down completely within seventy-two hours. Becca had seen it coming and firmly urged me to leave.

Because I had not had a chance to purchase a SIM card for my phone that would allow me to make phone calls, my husband had tried to reach the airline to reschedule my return flight for two days. The line was always busy. I spent those two days mostly in a hammock under a mango tree, which sounds ideal except that the fear and anxiety in the air kept rising until it was palpable.

Becca also tried to call the airline to rebook my ticket. After numerous attempts, she concluded that the airline had shut the phones down. She then tried the US Embassy and received only minimal information about "repatriation" that led her to believe that it could be prohibitively expensive, with no useful details. I would have to go to the embassy in person to find out more. The problem was that it was on the other side of the city and no one was supposed to be going anywhere.

Meanwhile, my husband called the travel insurance company. They covered evacuation and emergency expenses, and I thought it was worth alerting them to my situation. They were very helpful. They promised to help find a flight to get me home. They would call him back in six to eight hours. I didn't want to wait that long. By this time, I was near panic. It seemed to be better to try to purchase a new, one-way ticket and abandon the return ticket I had and try to cancel the original reservation later. I really did not have a lot of hope that there would be any seats available, but I decided to go online to try. Staying indefinitely did not seem to be wise for several reasons, but if I couldn't leave before the airport closed, that's what would happen.

To my great relief, there was room on a flight out the next day! I packed my suitcase, then tried to sleep. When I checked my messages at about 3 a.m., I learned that Emma had arranged for a private car to take me to the airport. Fortunately, I read that before I found out that all public transportation, including taxis and Grabs (the Filipino version of Uber), had been shut down at midnight! None of my friends in Manila owned cars at that time, so hiring someone to drive me was the only way.

My trip home was uneventful. While the short hop to Taipei was crowded, the longer leg to LA was only about a third full. Despite quite a few children and high emotions among many adults, it was quiet. I had a lot of time to reflect on my mixed emotions. Grateful to be going home, I was keenly aware that it was privilege that allowed me to do so. I felt I was betraying the solidarity I had for the people of the Philippines by being able to go home and leave them there to face whatever would happen next.

Effects of the Pandemic

Food shortages were expected. The deaths of many, many people living in poverty were feared with the specter of COVID-19 rampaging through the crowded neighborhoods and among those without homes.

A mere sixteen days after I left, food shortages were creating desperation. Hungry people with children to feed broke the law by going out to find food. Daily wage earners could not go to work so they had no money to buy what they needed. The church did all it could, but it was not even close to enough.

The government was not helping. Instead, President Rodrigo Duterte declared that anyone out in the streets could be shot for violating the order to stay home. This was a military response to a medical crisis, inappropriate to say the least. And ineffective at keeping desperate people from going outside. It amounted to an extension of the "war on drugs" in which people are shot and killed without any warrant or investigation. Both are, in fact, a "war on the poor," as many justice workers call it. A way for the government to look effective even though the problem remains unchanged.

The situation continued to get worse as COVID-19 continued to ramp up. Calls for mass testing went unheard, with the initial testing being restricted mostly to elected officials and other people with power. Medical care became harder to come by, with many people unable to afford it or access it when they needed it most. I have asthma and also some scarring in one lung; I was at high risk. Coming home meant that I could receive medical care if I needed it, but I was saddened, knowing the people there could not always get help.

My heart is with the people of the Philippines, always. My friends survived but too many others did not. Solidarity—it doesn't always mean staying. For me, it meant coming home so I wouldn't be eating food that someone else needed. Coming home also meant being able to send boxes filled with needed items. And it meant that I could let people know what the pandemic was like for people living in a different country. I was learning that deaconess/home missioners still keep serving the people in the face of the direst of circumstances.

Although this short trip was not the best beginning for writing this book, I was safe. There was no way to make progress writing until the pandemic passed, and I had no clue how long that was going to take. Like nearly everyone around the world, all I could do was wait. During the wait, I continued to wonder about where to find joy, how to keep serving, and so many other things that I wanted to learn from the deaconess/home missioners of the Philippines.

An Unexpected Step Forward

> But anyone who needs wisdom should ask God, whose very nature is to give to everyone without a second thought, without keeping score. Wisdom will certainly be given to those who ask. (Jas 1:5)

In the fall of 2020, I saw an ad on social media for a Doctor of Ministry (DMin) program at Pittsburgh Theological Seminary, a school I had never heard of before. I hadn't been looking for such a program. Years before, when my husband had encouraged me to get a DMin degree, I looked at several seminaries and hadn't found anything that appealed to me as a layperson. All of them were for clergy wanting to learn more about something pertinent to congregational ministry or their specific calling. I was not interested in any of those.

But this degree was in "Creative Writing and Public Theology"! It was the answer to my question, "How am I going to write that book?" It was also exactly what I wanted for my future (being a writer) and for the way I wanted to see myself (a public theologian). I sent in for more information about this program without finding out much about the school beyond knowing that it was connected to the Presbyterian Church. I was (and still am) sure God put that ad in front of me as a gift, but I managed to have the audacity to require that some contingencies be met before I applied. The main one was that this degree had to be paid for with scholarship money. I would not touch our retirement account for it. I applied for four scholarships, not knowing how much each one would grant.

The time for the first class came in June with no word from any of the scholarship committees. I know that scholarships are typically for the fall semester, so I went ahead with attending the class, figuring that I could find some way to pay for just the first one. During the one-week class, I received notification about one scholarship. The next followed a week later. The third soon after, with a fourth a month or so later. All were approved, the total amount so far above what I needed for the first year that I returned one and part of another and still had more than enough to cover not only tuition and fees, but also books, a new laptop, a writing desk, and an internet upgrade! God was speaking to me loud and clear!

When COVID vaccines became available early in 2021, hope poked its head up a bit further to convince me that I would, in fact, write this book, but still it would be two more years before I returned to the Philippines. When I did, I received another gift from God.

Easter in Pampanga

> Early in the morning of the first day of the week, while it was still dark, Mary Magdalene came to the tomb and saw that the stone had been taken away from the tomb. (John 20:1)

Fast-forward through the pandemic to spring 2023. Travel had been open for a while, but my schedule and family needs kept me home. Just a few days more than three years after I had run home to avoid lockdown in Manila, I finally boarded another plane. I was in the fourth semester of the DMin program, and I had learned a lot about writing and a few things about interviewing. It was time to get serious about writing this book.

As I began interviewing deaconess/home missioners, God had to help me be ready to learn from them. I had already learned something about the culture and the hardships during my previous trips. I had learned to love the people, with their openhanded hospitality and welcoming spirit. I knew they had a lot more to teach me. I intended to be an observer, a reporter, holding myself apart from involvement, knowing only that I love the Philippines and the people. I focused on the deaconess/home missioners because I am a deaconess. But it turned out that God knew another, deeper reason for this project, something I did not even suspect. I needed to learn something about myself. My travels were about to become a journey of the heart.

In several places in Scripture, we read that God hardens or softens someone's heart. Before I could learn the deepest lessons from my deaconess/home missioners (D/HM) siblings, God needed to soften my heart a bit. Learning is, at its core, transformation. Transformation is not possible if the heart is hard, even a little. God knew what I needed. It was God who arranged for me to be in Pampanga on Easter Sunday. It was Deaconess Bless de Leon and her friend, Julien Bolocon, who drove me there on Friday evening, and we spent most of Saturday at the church. I watched as the choir rehearsed and preparations were made for the next day.

Easter Sunday, 4 a.m., at Aldersgate United Methodist Church in Pampanga. The sky was still black. A rooster crowed, screeching "AlleLOOyah!" before the music started. The chairs that stretched back across the open area behind the sanctuary were lit by floodlights so that approximately five hundred people would be safe walking to their seats across the patchy grass in the dark. Again and again, the rooster crowed throughout the morning, "AlleLOOyah!" Each time, my spirit lifted higher, joining him in worship.

Waiting in the dark for worship to begin.

The praise band began playing, and the people, who had come from all over the area, four or five times more people than I am used to worshiping with, stood up around me, singing. I joined them. The temperature, never below 75°F, would start to rise, along with the sun, in about two hours. The sky became lighter so gradually that I didn't notice it until the floodlights were turned off. Worship continued for another two hours after the sun came over the tall trees behind us. Hymns were sung, prayers were prayed, the voices of children getting restless were heard in the quieter moments. The choir, directed by Deaconess Olga Ducut, sang "The Hallelujah Chorus" beautifully, with tremendous spirit and energy, and many in the congregation joined in. A sermon was preached, entitled "We Find Our Hope in the Resurrection." More speaking, more praying than I am used to. People came forward to give their offerings and to give their lives to Christ, either for the first time or to renew their commitment. That isn't often a part of worship at my church. Deaconesses were among those praying for them.

8 a.m. After four hours of worship, the temperature was on its way to being very warm.

The congregation in prayer. Many have gone to the front for individual prayers.

I am accustomed to worship services lasting about an hour, but on this Easter Sunday, four hours did not seem taxing or boring or too long. When the benediction was spoken, my heart was full, my spirit renewed, and my heart softened by the Spirit-filled worship. Resurrection felt real, a liberation from darkness. Full-hearted joy.

I had expected a lovely service where I witnessed with my own eyes what deaconesses do on the highest holy day of the year. It was so much more. I have been attending worship on Easter Sundays my entire life. My faith was strong enough to lead me across the ocean to pursue my calling, but it turns out I was just a bit jaded, a bit—not exactly cynical—but a bit distanced from the miracle of Easter. I see now that my heart was just a little bit hard. I thought I was there to observe and interview deaconesses, not to learn the heart of what Easter was about. I am not saying I didn't know, but I had lost touch with how it felt, how the heart instead of the head knows the resurrection is real. I had not expected to be so moved, so transformed in my beliefs about the way I expect worship to be. I am not accustomed to seeing so many people go forward to ask for prayer, to being surrounded by hundreds of people praying, singing, responding with all of themselves to the good news that Jesus Christ is alive. To realize that, in the midst of serious challenges throughout our world and within our United Methodist denomination, so many could be of one heart in worshiping the Savior of us all was so much more than I anticipated. It was what I needed to restore my hope and heal from the loneliness and doubt of the pandemic. Such a gift, this awakening on Easter morning. My heart was transformed and ready to learn. I am grateful.

I learned that celebrating Easter for hours and hours is a gift of joy because the resurrection is real, and it is new even when you have celebrated it several dozen times in your life. I experienced Jesus coming to us brand-new on Easter morning. My spirit still continues to echo the rooster today:

"AlleLOOyah!" Amen!

4

The Order of Deaconess/Home Missioners (DHM)

> Who is qualified for this kind of ministry? We aren't like so many people who hustle the word of God to make a profit. We are speaking through Christ in the presence of God, as those who are sincere and as those who are sent from God. (2 Cor 2:16b–17)

When I first traveled to the Philippines in 2017, the deaconesses I met were surprised that I was about to become a "new" deaconess at my gray-haired age. In addition, I was often asked questions about education, since they had heard that only five classes are required to become a deaconess/home missioner in the US. They didn't know that we are required to have a bachelor's degree before we begin our training. There are several other significant differences in the ways the Order of Deaconess/Home Missioner is administered in the two countries. Part of my purpose, then, not only in this book, but in other interactions with deaconess/home missioners on both sides of the Pacific, became to clear up misconceptions and confusion. But before I could teach others, there was more I needed to learn.

Harris Memorial College (HMC), south of Manila in Taytay, and Southern Philippines Methodist Colleges, Inc. (SPMCI), in

Kidapawan in the Cotabato region of the southernmost island of Mindanao, are the training schools for deaconess/home missioners. Graduating classes call each other "batchmates," an appropriate term for people who have been formed and educated together in tight-knit groups, usually between the ages of sixteen through twenty-one. Their bonds remain close throughout their lives. The curriculum is demanding, and the daily routine is strict. As a result, deaconess/home missioners are "Never Unprepared" (Harris' motto) and very self-disciplined. The future demands of ministry will not easily overwhelm them. They earn their bachelor's degrees at the same time they are meeting the requirements for becoming deaconesses and home missioners. They major in early childhood education, kindergarten, or elementary education. To be prepared for anything they might be called on to do, they are also, regardless of major, required to learn to play piano or organ, to direct a choir, and to sing in harmony, whether or not they are musically inclined. They live in a dormitory, a dozen students in each dormitory room, with a shared bathroom down the hall. They are required to keep their area neat, making their beds and putting their personal items away before going to an early breakfast. From them, I learned that self-discipline gives strength, determination, and the confidence that they can handle anything.

During the summers, they are assigned to internships in churches. This gives them an opportunity to put what they have been taught into practice and solidify what they have learned. Serving in a church is the best way to know what it's like to be a deaconess/home missioner.

When they finish their education at Harris or SPMCI, they are consecrated by a bishop and appointed to ministry in a specific congregation. These appointments are the same as the appointments that United Methodist clergy receive from a bishop. They are made annually and typically take effect from July 1 to June 30. An appointment may be renewed to return to the same place, or it may be changed to another church or position. This can mean moving from place to place as often as every year. Most appointments are to serve local churches. Because many United Methodist churches in the Philippines also have a weekday school connected with them, teaching and/or directing those schools is often part of the appointment. In addition, they may be required to direct the choir, play a keyboard, write liturgy, and more. Deaconess/home missioners are well prepared by their educations to take on whatever tasks are needed at their churches.

Deaconesses Emelyn Castillo (our host), Emma Cantor (my guide), School Registrar Michelle Salado, and myself in front of the administration building at SPMCI.

Other deaconess/home missioners are appointed to a special (or "not-typical") assignment. Some are assigned to be on the faculty or staff of a United Methodist school that is not connected with a congregation to serve at any grade level, including college. Others are appointed to work for the United Methodist Philippines Regional Conference on one of the boards or agencies or in some other capacity. Some work at the denominational level of The United Methodist Church for one of the general boards or agencies. Some work at the National Council of Churches Philippines. And there are other appointments, including overseas missionary work. In the Philippines, deaconess/home missioners are flexible and gifted in many ways.

In the United States, candidates for deaconess/home missioner are required to have a bachelor's degree before beginning their education, which is, as the deaconess/home missioners in the Philippines had heard, five classes: Theology of Mission, Old Testament, New Testament, United Methodist History, and United Methodist Polity. There are other requirements, such as working with a mentor and being part of a book study/accountability group. We have not all been trained as teachers, but some of us have teaching credentials. Others are nurses. There is a wide diversity of other callings as well, including leading a specialized ministry, working for a nonprofit organization, serving as an inclusion specialist for a school district, and many more. Unlike in the Philippines, US appointments are not at the discretion of the local bishop. Instead, as part of our annual report to the Deaconess/Home Missioner Office (which is under United Women in Faith), we ask to be appointed to work we have found or are looking for ourselves. The office either approves of our choice as meeting their requirements or encourages us to find something more suitable. The bishop is then notified of the appointment, who confirms it when they commission us to that work.

I also learned that the differences in our preparation do not mean that there is a difference in our hearts. On both sides of the Pacific (in fact, in every place in the world where there are United Methodist deaconess/home missioners), we all follow the same four mandates to "alleviate suffering, eradicate causes of injustice and all that robs life of dignity and worth, facilitate the development of full human potential, and share in the building of global community through the church universal."[1] Each of us lives those mandates out, and together we make a difference in the church and in the world.

1. United Methodist Church, *Book of Discipline*, para. 1913.1.

Interlude

The City

> Promote the welfare of the city where I have sent you into exile. Pray to the Lord for it because your future depends on its welfare. (Jer 29:7)

In the Metro Manila area, as in the greater Los Angeles area, it is impossible to tell when you have traveled from one municipality to another. Parts of the downtown area are very old. Intramuros, for example, was built in 1571, during Spain's rule. Elsewhere, there are modern skyscrapers being built next to buildings built soon after World War II. Residential areas are mostly small lots, with very little room between homes. Shared walls are common, especially in the poorer neighborhoods, where building materials are diverse and appear to be scavenged.

Traffic is often jammed. On streets with four lanes marked, there are typically six or even seven cars side by side. Motorcycles and bicycles pass in the narrow spaces between them. When traffic is stop-and-go, my heart often skips a beat when I see vendors, including young children who are sometimes carrying babies, going between cars trying to make sales. How often do two-wheeled vehicles collide with vendors? I have never seen it happen, but it must sometimes. Driving in Metro Manila traffic requires a decisive and brave personality. Hesitation could easily result in never getting to your destination. There are several other options available for transportation. Jeepneys are a form of public transportation created by stretching World War II US Army Jeeps to bus length. Passengers sit sideways, facing each other on benches running from front to back, holding as many people as can squeeze in. Colorfully painted, with religious or other phrases proclaiming the beliefs of the owners, they don't have glass windows or back doors, just empty openings.

Jeepneys are a colorful, low-cost means of transportation.

When it rains, plastic sheeting is lowered on the sides. Jeepneys are the least expensive way to commute, costing less than ten pesos (less than twenty cents) to ride the long length of an avenue. Vans are a step up, having the same front-to-back configuration, but providing more protection from the elements. For those who can afford them, there are taxis and rideshare "Grab" cars. There are several urban train lines. Buses are another option, with many running from the city to the provinces (countryside). Some are more luxurious than others.

5

Interviews

"I WANT TO MEET every deaconess in every place in the Philippines." That's what I said to Emma when we first spoke about this book. She was excited about the idea, but she very gently let me know how unrealistic that was. I scaled back my ambitions and instead decided to interview a reasonable number of deaconess/home missioners in diverse settings, with different callings/appointments, and representing a range of ages.

In 2023, I made two trips to the Philippines, one in March/April and one in November, for about three weeks each time. I interviewed in Quezon City, in downtown Manila at United Methodist Headquarters, in Santiago City, Isabela (North-Central Luzon), in Davao City, and throughout the Cotabato region, both in Mindanao. Twenty-eight interviews all told. I also attended nearly a dozen events. All of this expanded my knowledge about deaconess/home missioners, as well as my understanding of what it means to be consecrated to a lifetime of love, justice, and service. It also showed me how to improve at building relationships and how to be in solidarity with others while serving God.

Call Stories

> "It's not just the church who needs us, but the world!"—
> Deaconess Maria Jessica R. Cecilio

God rarely speaks clearly to me. Most of the time the guidance God gives me looks like a series of doors, some open and some closed, not written or spoken words. After some initial hesitation, I go through one open door, and then another and another. Before I became a deaconess, I was looking for a community of justice-minded people to belong to that included people who understood helping people with disabilities belong in church was a justice issue. I was longing for more people to know about the important work I was part of, the Disability Ministries Committee of The United Methodist Church and the California-Pacific Disability Ministries Task Force. I believed that would be more likely to happen if I were part of a church organization. And then God opened a door, showing me that deaconesses existed, and then continuing to pique my interest until I went to an informational event to learn more. At every step after that I thought I would find a closed door, but I never did. I finally went through the final door to be consecrated as a deaconess.

As I heard call stories during the interviews with the deaconess/home missioners in the Philippines, I paid close attention. Their stories were something like mine, but, of course, also different.

Deaconess Mimi (Karmina) Lopez, serving at Puno United Methodist Church in Quezon City, told me she felt called to full-time deaconess service at Christmas Institute in 2009 when she was nineteen or twenty. Christmas Institute is an annual event for youth held for several days after Christmas each year. It is led by deaconess/home missioners, who teach the youth about God, and what it means to be a Christian. Every year some respond to God's call to full-time service, and Mimi was one of them. She said, "I cannot explain," when I asked how she knew she was called. She just knew, she said. As a young girl, she had already been influenced by her *Lolo* (grandfather), who served as the pastor of the church she and her family attended in the Metro Manila area, so she was ready to respond to the call when it came. Unlike me, but just like every deaconess/home missioner in the Philippines, she had known about deaconesses since she was a child. And she knew she was called, while for me, I was not sure until I was almost at the end of the process.

Left to right: Deaconesses Michelle Dudang-Ortiz, myself, Mimi Lopez, and Elijah Alivia-Layugan

Deaconess Michelle Dudang-Ortiz heard God's call at seventeen years old. She had grown up admiring the commitment of the deaconesses she saw, how they were always at church. She told me, "As a deaconess now, I give back to the Lord what he has done for me. That is my 'how to worship the Lord' in my service, in my dedication as a deaconess. Because I know this is his will for me to be a deaconess in the church, so I give all, even my time, my resources, toward the church."

I heard and saw this commitment from everybody I interviewed. Being a deaconess/home missioner is not something any of them do partway or part time. It is who they are. Even though I had not used the phrase, "I give back to the Lord what he has done for me," I felt it ring in my heart when Michelle said it. I am all in, just as Michelle is.

My experience of being called at an older age was different from all the deaconess/home missioners I interviewed. Being called as a teen was the norm for them, and a few had begun thinking about a future as a deaconess at an even younger age. Deaconess Norma Dollaga said, "I was eight years when I started to contemplate" being a deaconess. "And then when I started at Harris, I felt that the fulfillment of the heart is becoming true."

Deaconess Jessica Cecilio was also eight years old when her pastor told her, "I think you can be a good deaconess someday," but she did not feel called yet. Later, as a teen, she already loved teaching children, but she did not decide to become a deaconess until she was sixteen. Very early one morning, she woke up crying. "I'm crying so hard, but I don't know why. Then suddenly I started to reflect on the life I'm living. Then I felt something inside me that's talking to me and telling me that . . . I want to offer my life to God through service through serving him, and the first thing that comes in my mind is the deaconess ministry." She realized "there are many things I can do to serve God, but I feel like deaconess ministry is what I am called for and what God wants me to do."

There was one catch. Her father did not want her to become a deaconess. He wanted her to become a nurse, so she took entrance exams for several schools in an effort to be an obedient daughter. However, she said, "Maybe God wanted me to be at Harris [the deaconess/home missioner training school], so he closed all the doors for me, and opened the door for Harris. So, my father will not have a choice but to send me to Harris." This is an unusually clear path set before her. Most call stories are not this definite, except that this one meshes with my own experience. Other doors closed to me as well, until the one labeled "Deaconess" opened. Like Jessica, I had only one choice and that was deaconess.

Each call story is unique, but there are similarities for deaconess/home missioners in the Philippines. All of them were familiar with deaconesses, loved children, and wanted to serve God. Some of them told me that they chose deaconess/home missioner instead of clergy because they wanted to teach children. This calling is a good fit for them.

There is one more story I want to tell you, one that has a different ending. It was told to me by Coleen Capuno, who was a deaconess appointed to Friendship United Methodist Church, near Pampanga, about an hour north of Manila.

When Coleen was in her second year of her deaconess education at Harris Memorial College, some of her "big sisters" (students ahead of her in school) came to her in the school laundry one day. One of them said to her, "Hey, little sister, I think you're lying."

"What?" she replied. "Wh-what? Why do you think I'm lying?"

"You will not be a deaconess," the big sister told her. "I think you're going to be a pastor."

Others told her the same thing. Coleen remembers thinking, "I think maybe this big sister, she's seeing something, or maybe the Lord is putting something in her." Later, when she was appointed to a church as a student deaconess, some of the church members kept taking her hand and pressing the back of it to their forehead, a gesture which is used to ask a pastor for a blessing, and saying, "Hello, Pastor!" This was in a church that is very familiar with deaconesses. She corrected them, saying, "I'm not a pastor. I'm a student deaconess." This felt to her like further affirmation that she was called to ordained ministry.

She went on to serve as a deaconess for four years, but the call to ordination remained strong. She finally left the order and went to seminary. She was in her final year when I interviewed her. Now she is Reverend Coleen Caputo, still serving in The United Methodist Church, but now as clergy. Her call to ministry was certain, but it was to ordained ministry, not to serving as a deaconess. My heart jumped when I heard her story because my own journey had led me in the opposite direction. I had begun by seeking ordination and later found that deaconess is my calling.

How Do You Serve?

I sat down in a chair near the front of the beautiful little sanctuary, noticing the beautiful flowers, palm fronds, and other Palm Sunday decorations, listening to the voices around me. Voices of children, youth, and adults who sounded excited and happy. Once or twice a little one became upset but was quickly soothed. As I sat alone, people occasionally came to greet me, but it was a busy day, and no one stayed long.

On this trip to the Philippines, I wanted to observe deaconesses in action, to learn as much as I could about how to be a deaconess not only by interviewing many of them, but by watching them. As I watched, I tried to keep track of Deaconess Elijah Alivia-Layugan, who had taken nearly an hour of her time on this busy Sunday to drive across town to pick me up and bring me to church. I listened for her voice and tried to watch what she did, but she was in and out of the room several times. She made sure the youngest and the oldest members were taken care of. She rehearsed the choir. She checked in with the young adults and the youth and corralled the children at least once. She also introduced me to several members of the congregation.

As worship began, I didn't know where Elijah was. Taking care of something somewhere. When it came time for the anthem, she was there, directing the choir. Then I didn't see her again until the children came forward to participate in the sacrament of Holy Communion. Then once again she left the room until the sermon was over, when I saw her peeking in at the side entrance to the front of the church. When the benediction was over, she came to the center to make the announcements.

After worship she was taking care of . . . the children? The youth? Elderly members? I wasn't sure, but I was busy talking to people who wanted to know more about why I was there. Soon enough, I heard Elijah say, "Let's have some lunch. Follow me!"

and we went to eat lunch with the leaders of the church in a cool room behind the sanctuary. As we ate and talked with everyone, I was thinking about how much Elijah had done that morning. Such incredible energy and stamina!

And she wasn't finished! As we left the church, she asked, "Do you need anything? We can go to the mall." As a matter of fact, I did need a couple of things, so we went, bringing another friend. They both patiently waited as I tried things on and even brought me different sizes until I found what I wanted. And *then* as an added treat, we went to a little restaurant for *halo-halo* (pronounced with "a" as in "hat"). You may not know what *halo-halo* is, so I will tell you. It looks sort of like a milkshake but when you look more closely, it's more like a snow cone with very soft ice and something delicious and creamy and fruity in the middle, maybe flavored sweetened condensed milk. You stir it all up and enjoy. It might be purple (ube) or turquoise blue (I don't know what flavor that was) or pale orange/yellow (banana crème, I think), or many other colors. Every single one delicious. How do I know that? Well, I will let you guess.

I am sure that Deaconess Elijah is just as generous with her time with everybody else. In fact, that afternoon, since she is among the minority of church workers who own a car, she picked up a carload of people and took them wherever they needed to go.

How does Elijah serve? In every way needed, and then she goes above and beyond that, doing things that make people happy and feel loved.

Deaconess Elijah is not the only deaconess who works hard serving others, and Palm Sunday is not the only day of the year that requires that much energy. I am certain every deaconess/home missioner puts that much energy into their work. Spending time with deaconess/home missioners has taught me that they all work really hard and still they often radiate joy!

But I also learned that I was very interested in what deaconess/home missioners had to tell me. Some of them were nervous about being interviewed, and, at the beginning, I was nervous about interviewing them. As I learned how to relax, I also figured out how to put people at ease, and that led to building a relationship with them, a relationship that is continued with some on social media. For all of them, I will always remember where we were when we met, how their faces glowed when they told me something important to them, and how they met challenges with deep faith and the solid preparation their education and training had provided. They are my deaconess/home missioner siblings, my *kapatid*.

Interlude

Juxtaposition

In the Philippines, everything looks beautiful.
Trees are greener than green.

Flowers and fruit are abundant, growing within easy reach,
scenting the air.

Vegetables grow easily. Laughter is heard often.
Music is sweet and ubiquitous.

You think you are in Paradise, until you listen to the people.

They tell stories about husbands and sons being shot in the street

or even while sitting on their porch

by masked gunmen who ride motorcycles at night
with the headlights off.

No investigation is ever done, no arrests ever made.

You might think that the dead men must be guilty of something

until you hear a prisoner in a county jail talk about
police invading her home

in the middle of the night while she was asleep in bed

with her husband and four children under the age of ten.

Her husband was arrested at the same time,
leaving the children alone.

The charges didn't come for weeks or even months[1]

and then they were "possession of illegal explosives,"
supposedly under their pillows,

in the bed they share with their children.

And you might still believe those charges,
maintaining the illusion of Paradise,

believing that these parents would endanger their own children,

until you hear very similar stories from many other prisoners,

who were all social workers or community organizers
helping the poor.

Some were teaching indigenous women to read,
some were healthcare workers,

and more than one was a pastor taking care
of church members and

following Christ's commands.

As Paradise's appearance turns shabby,
marred by blood and corruption,

the stories get worse. Attorneys for the accused are

murdered on their porches or just outside their offices.

Their widows are threatened to be quiet
"or else your children will be orphans."

Eventually, you begin to see the trees are not so green
and the fruit is rotten.

The farmers no longer have land for planting vegetables

to feed their own starving families because
large corporations now own it all.

During the pandemic, people cannot work or buy food.

Children cry for rice.

1. The Constitution of the Philippines is very similar to the US Constitution. It is unconstitutional not to inform a prisoner what they are charged with.

Desperate people violate the strict lockdown to

find a way to relieve the children's hunger,
to bring even a bit of food home.

They are arrested or shot for breaking the curfew.

When, finally, the vaccine arrives, at first it is not for everyone,

only the rich and powerful.

The poor have to wait.

When they get sick, they can't afford doctors,

so they treat COVID symptoms with over-the-counter medicine.

If they can't afford that,

stay home and pray.

In the poorest homes, shacks made of
scavenged wood and sheet metal,

everyone in the house is soon sick because

there is only one room, only one bed for all to share.

Death comes in and bodies are carried out.

Through the streets and alleys, over the mountains and the rivers,

come the deaconesses, church workers who serve the poor,

the widowed, the marginalized, the children,

teaching, singing, praying, loving,

bringing the light that is hope.

How Do You Keep Going in the Face of Great Injustice?

> He has told you, human one, what is good, and to do justice, embrace faithful love, and walk humbly with your God. (Mic 6:8)

Focused on the needs of the poor and the powerless, Deaconesses Norma P. Dollaga and Rubylin Litao are serving under special appointment by the bishop to the Ecumenical Center for Development. In this role, they lead two nonprofit organizations: Dambana, which brings food, medicine, clothing, a listening ear, prayer, and worship to the poor, and Rise Up for Life and for Rights, which empowers women who have lost husbands, sons, fathers, and brothers to the war on drugs (in reality, a war on the poor), training them to support and advocate for each other. I initially met these two women on my first trip to the Philippines. They spoke about Rise Up at the National Council of Churches offices and brought some of the women they were helping. Together they make a powerful team, with gifts and strengths that complement each other while they comfort, bring hope, empower, and motivate. Unfortunately, when I interviewed Norma, Rubylin was away to minister to people affected by an oil spill in Mindoro. I am grateful that Norma could find time for me.

It is because of Deaconess Norma that I have learned a little about indigenous religion. She is called *Diwata*, which means "fairy." The implication is that she has the spirit of the ancestors or nature spirits and is worthy of respect as a result. She is also referred to as a *babaylan*. Before Europeans came to the Philippines, *babaylan* were leaders, mostly women, who had the ability to communicate with the spirit world. They also had the gifts of healing, foretelling, and insight.[1] Norma has those gifts and so, too, do many of her colleagues, who are also called *babaylan* and *diwata*. I thank her and the others for inspiring me to learn more and to open my thinking to new understandings of God.

She seems ageless. That is, I cannot guess her age. I can only say that she is older than thirty and younger than I am, because she calls me "*ate*," which means "older sister."

Slender and energetic, with a beautiful smile and a sly sense of humor, she sometimes greets me by engaging me in a short dance. This is one indication of her gifts, because I am an unskilled and reluctant dancer, and yet I try to dance with her. Her naturally curly hair is always pulled neatly back. Even during typhoons, when she has been walking through flooded streets, she rarely looks untidy. I attribute this to the fact that she really is a fairy, a *diwata*. She laughs easily, finding something funny about herself or about the situation or even (kindly) about me. Her laughter is contagious.

But there are times when Norma flashes with anger at injustice. And she cries sometimes, feeling the pain of others. She sees troubles caused by corruption, troubles too hard to bear—sickness, neglect, starvation, murder, deep grief. She does not always have enough food to bring to all the poor, not enough medicine or vitamins to distribute to the poorly fed prisoners, not enough comfort to bring to the mothers and wives of men shot in the streets. It is because of her and others like her that I know of the hardships of living in the Philippines. It is because we have cried together, laughed together, danced together, and been angry at injustice together that we are true sisters.

I would follow *Diwata* Norma anywhere, but I do not have fairy wings. In darkness her light shines more brightly. In difficult circumstances she seems to walk more lightly, barely touching the ground. She seems closer to heaven, and she brings heaven closer to us through her poetic prayers and liturgies. When I am with

1. Strobel, *Babaylan*, 13.

her, I feel Jesus in the room. The *babaylan diwata* brings her gifts to many, and I am grateful.

I asked Norma if she has ever wanted to quit. The needs and the challenges are endless, it seems to me. Insurmountable. I remember that Jesus said, "The poor you will always have with you," and I wondered—how long can you continue to serve like this if you are called to do the same thing over and over and not see any progress? I asked her if she ever feels like giving up and letting someone else do the work. She was surprised, maybe even shocked at the question, I think because it was so far outside of her thinking. Her immediate response was eloquent enough, but, as she thought about it later, her poetic spirit came even more alive and she sent me this:

"I Am Not Strong," by Deaconess Norma P. Dollaga

"I am not strong
If not for the tears of the poor
Like a river passing through the rocks that will
Lead the waves to the shore of freedom

I am not strong
If not for the wings of people ready to soar
Like eagles that fly the widest horizon and
Worship the beauty of sunset and sunrise
The light, the power, the
Fire, the truth, the redemption and liberation

I am not strong
If not for the movement of hope and struggle
The courage that is never depleted by storms
But the will to carry on until justice is done

Like the earth ready to nurture the seeds of hope,

Ready to weep as the seeds die but in the spring
of ever-changing season

The flowers bloom, dancing with the wind and stars above.

In this journey,

I learn the ways of hope and grace

And unlearn the ways of regret and giving up.

I must confess,

I am not strong

Many times afraid

to dip my feet into the currents of a river of tears

of the downtrodden

to spread my wings and dance with the wind of the people's
movement

and to bury a thousand deaths in the womb of the earth

But what is this that leads me,

but the Ruah,

the Love known and shared

Not because I am LOVE

but because

LOVE has shared its grace to me."

(© 2023, Norma P. Dollaga. Used with permission)

This poem answers how to keep going in the face of great injustice. It helps me articulate the reason I keep returning to the Philippines when I could just stay home. It's because I find strength there, ways to overcome my fears, the courage to do what needs to be done. I also feel that Christ is with me and in the hearts of the people. It's also because the Holy Spirit is with me as I travel.

The Philippine culture is clear in this poem in the images of nature and the way she couples them with the values of the people. When she writes, "Like a river passing through the rocks that will/ Lead the waves to the shore of freedom," her words express the dreams, hopes, and prayers of the people as they join those of many others working to lead others to freedom. It's also reminiscent of Scriptures that tell us "a little child shall lead them" and "the last shall be first," as the smaller river joins the larger ocean. There are only a few people showing many others the way out of the oppression and hardships of the Philippines, and yet, the impact is felt.

There are also echoes of the indigenous religion which finds the holy in nature and holds the relationship between human and environment as sacred. Norma is strongly Christian but with a perspective that is deep and ancient. Her faith is less about self and more about community, more creation-centered, and more sensory than I have typically experienced. Her words here and in her liturgy that she has shared elsewhere have resulted in a profound change in the way I believe. It feels heart-centered as opposed to the head-centered variety I learned in seminary and have experienced too often in church. Retired Deaconess Rebecca Asedillo, who served in the Philippines and now lives in the US, wrote in the book *Rice in the Storm* that interactions between God and humans are not theoretical, in the realm of thought and ideas, but instead they are experiences with God, something we are immersed in with our whole selves, that are not necessarily rational, but nevertheless real.[2] This is where Norma's written words take me, into a place where I feel God's presence and stop trying to understand, a place where I experience a mystery that I don't need to find an answer to. This is why I want to continue my travels to the Philippines. I experience God in a much deeper way there.

I interviewed Norma in the spring of 2023, and in the fall of that year, I had my first opportunity to attend an all-day Rise Up training in person, to see Deaconesses Norma and Rubylin in action.

2. Asedillo, "When Did We See," 132.

Deaconess Norma Dollaga listening intently to a woman at the Rise Up event.

Rise Up for Life and for Rights is a United Methodist organization connected with the National Council of Churches Philippines. It is run with the assistance of ecumenical partners, including Sister Eleanor Llanes, ICM, and my friend at Decker House, Rebecca Lawson. The purpose of Rise Up is to train and empower women who have lost husbands, sons, and brothers to the government's war on drugs. The dead are victims of extrajudicial killings, shot in the streets or on their front porches by masked men riding tandem on unmarked motorcycles at night with the headlights off. No investigations are ever completed. No one is ever held accountable.

When Rubylin and Norma arrive in a community after an extrajudicial killing, the immediate needs of the grieving women for prayer and comfort are met. Then, if the women are interested, they are taught to help each other, to organize and share their stories of the injustice that took their loved ones from them. This gives the women strength and purpose. It helps them find their way through their grief. I was nearly overwhelmed by how many women attended. Just thinking of their collective pain made me emotional. Starting with breakfast and ending late in the afternoon with each woman receiving a bag of rice, their need for physical food bracketed the spiritual and emotional nourishment they received.

In between, many of them followed breakfast by attending the Roman Catholic Mass in the sanctuary upstairs. After returning downstairs, they heard a reflection on the story of the walk to Emmaus, then created art that demonstrated the ways that the passage was relevant to their own lives. Their work showed where they were in the process of healing. Each person shared with the entire group, telling the story of what they had drawn, some with tears, others with determination, many of them also expressing gratitude for the work of Rise Up! It was a time of healing and growth.

Rubylin then spoke words of healing and comfort. Norma followed that with what felt to me like a pep rally, strengthening the women for their work of supporting one another. These two are a wonderful team, Rubylin being quiet and reassuring, and Norma helping others find their courage and power with exhortations punctuated by orchestrated handclaps, both grounded in deep compassion.

Energized, the group then lined up outside, each one holding a photo of their loved one. They marched together to the columbarium of the church, where deceased church members were interred all around them. They placed their photos along the low walls and lit a candle in front of each one, spending time in prayer and finding closure. When they returned to the hall, it was time for a final word before cleaning up, receiving their rice, and leaving for home in jeepneys and vans.

It had been a busy, hot day. I am grateful that I was able to see Norma and Rubylin in action, glimpsing the difference they have made in the lives of so many women by helping them process grief and teaching them to help others who had also experienced loss, helping them to heal emotionally and spiritually, and listening to them deeply, with compassion and empathy.

This is how deaconesses keep going in the face of challenges—they create a community that cares for one another, where they find healing while they help others to heal. They empower each other and others by helping each other to remember that the power and love of God is at work in the world through their hands and feet and hearts. In this, I find an extension of solidarity, with added strength stemming from relationships and collaboration between coworkers who are building God's kin-dom. Even more than that, this kind of deep caring is loving others as we love ourselves. The shared identity, this "self in the other," is called "*kapwa*."[3] The word for God's inmost self and, by extension, our shared identity with God is "*loob*." These Tagalog terms are relational and foundational, an important part of who they are as Filipinos. The communal nature of their culture is expressed in these words, words that are not comprehensible to those of us who live in the individualistic culture of the United States. We have much to learn here. The way deaconess/home missioners keep going in difficult times is found within the connectedness of these words, connected to each other and connected to God, knowing that what affects one affects all and that God is in their midst—I believe this is the strength that allows them to have hope enough to continue on working for God's justice, compassion, and grace in the hardest of times.

3. Strobel, *Babaylan*, 52.

What Gives You Joy?

Before I even asked this question, I listened hard to learn where hard-working, dedicated deaconess/home missioners found joy. For some, joy lit their faces as they spoke about children learning about Jesus. Others struggled with the question, spending time to ponder as they spoke. It appeared they hadn't even thought about it before and had trouble naming what gives them joy. I could relate to the second group too well.

During the pandemic, it had been difficult for me to find joy or even, at times, the presence of God, so I was asking what gave the deaconess/home missioners joy for a deeply personal reason. They had lived through the pandemic, just as the rest of the world had. They had faced the challenges of meeting the many needs of the people during a global crisis. Even in more typical times, serving people who live in extreme poverty or who have lost loved ones to extrajudicial killings or who have lost everything they have to earthquake, flood, landslide, or other hardships seems like it would be impossible. And yet the people I interviewed told me they find joy and fulfillment in serving. Their stories have helped me find more joy in my own life.

Let me begin telling their stories this way.

Without exception, every deaconess and home missioner I interviewed loves children. In fact, most of them told me that they answered the call to ministry so that they could serve God by teaching children. It is their goal, their passion, to teach little children to read and write, but most of all to teach them to know Jesus.

The majority serve in that way six—and, for some of them, seven—days each week, barely finding time off to spend with their friends and family, to rest and relax. In fact, the most difficult question for many of them to answer is "What do you do for Sabbath rest? To rest and renew?" Is rest a way to find joy? I wondered. Some, most notably in Mindanao, seemed not to understand if I used the term "time off" as I asked the question. I don't think this is a language barrier. I think it's a cultural barrier. At the same time, many said they found their greatest joy in teaching children, that this is the reason they serve. Perhaps they don't understand "time off" because they find such joy in their work. They light up when talking about the children. Some of them bubble over with laughter when talking about teaching. Some who are appointed to other ways of serving told me they missed teaching the children, even when they are very good at what they are currently doing.

Deaconess Ruth Trube is among those who miss teaching. She is now serving the urban poor in the Davao Episcopal Area in Mindanao because that is where the bishop has appointed her. She finds the transience of the people to be a challenge. As soon as she and her coworkers get a program set up in one area, the people they are trying to serve have moved on. While she misses working with children, she tells me that she finds hope and joy in serving this way.

Deaconess Ruth Trube and myself

She feels "that God is walking before me because for various ministries that I face challenges, I surpass it all, I surpass it although it is one step at a time, but when I reach the finish line, I felt that God has walked before me, reaching that goal." What a powerful vision—the certainty of God walking before her! It is God who has reached the goal, and she is following. She serves because she finds God in it, and in God she finds joy! And that joy shows as she talks about following God this way. I am grateful to learn this from Deaconess Ruth! This image has found a home in my heart that will give me joy for the rest of my life.

Some deaconess/home missioners who have been appointed to school administration have managed to remain in the classroom part time. They find their time with the children or young adults brings them the joy they need to provide a balance with the paperwork and stress of the office work. Sharing God's love with children and young people is the reason they became deaconess/home missioners, and while they understand the necessity of having someone to run a school, their joy is found in the classroom.

While in the Cotabato region of Mindanao, I visited with three school administrators, Deaconess Gemma Labagan at J. L. Valencia School (K–5) in Polomolok, Deaconess Christine DeGuzman-Cortado at Greene Academy (K–12) in Makilala, and Deaconess Michelle Salado, registrar and faculty member at Southern Philippines Methodist Colleges, Inc. (a training college for deaconess/home missioners as well as a seminary) in Kidapawan. Both Gemma and Christine rather ruefully reminded me that their training did not include a school administration major. Of the many tasks that their education and training prepared them for, this was not one of them.

Deaconess Gemma does not feel qualified to do this work, but she opened the previously closed J. L. Valencia School by starting with a kindergarten class, and has successful grown the school by one grade level each year. She had previously served as a missionary in Taiwan, teaching basic English in high school and college, even though she was a preschool major. She tells me that, on paper, she is not qualified to be a school administrator, so she is not quite sure why she was chosen to do this. She finds every day a challenge, and says "I want to teach children, not to run the school, but

I'm doing what I can, so for now that's my goal. I hope my service can revive again the school." Her goal to bring the school back to full capacity is what she was appointed to do, but teaching is what brings her joy. She is still teaching in the mornings, but this leaves a lot of work to do in the afternoons and during some evenings. If she says anything to her supervisor about having too much work and that she needs an assistant, the response is that she could stop teaching. She is adamant that she would rather stop being the administrator. From Gemma I learned that even when you feel you are not qualified, you can still be very effective, and that sometimes even if you are firm when asking for what it is that brings you joy, it is necessary to compromise. Professional goals are good, but what makes your heart happy is nonnegotiable.

Deaconess Christine DeGuzman-Cortado is the registrar at Greene Academy, a K–12 school in Makilala. Like Gemma, she teaches in addition to her administrative duties. When I asked what gives her joy, she began by referring to her family, an answer many others gave as well.

Deaconesses Christine DeGuzman-Cortado, Emelyn Castillo, Emma Cantor, and Janisa Bole-Galeos at Greene Academy

"The most joy is being with my family, because we love to travel," she began, saying that she and her husband (a pastor who also teaches at the academy) and their teenaged daughter drive up into the mountains every weekend, living in a community with a population that is 98 percent indigenous people. They work alongside[4] the community members, helping them and inviting them to come to church and Sunday school. They also spend holidays and special occasions in this community, finding it "somehow relaxing" for them to have a life away from school. They began this way of life when they taught at SPMCI. At that time, they felt distanced from the community outside the school and asked themselves how they could teach effectively about how to serve communities when they lived at the college, apart from the community. Spending weekends and holidays in the mountain community became their way of grounding themselves and being authentic in what they were teaching. Since that time, they have transferred to Greene Academy (which is not far from SPMCI), and they continue to live in the indigenous community on the weekends.

Some of the children there had come from other communities that had been red-tagged[5] and bombed. "I have a small child," Christine told me,

> three or four years old. When she heard a helicopter, the sound of a helicopter around, she's really scared. . . . I asked the mother, "What happened to make this little girl act like this?" The mother told me that "the military bombed their houses because there are rebels in there." I asked the mother, "Did she see what happened?" and she said yes. There were other children, most of them older, who could not sleep and would take cover anywhere they could for the same reason.

Deaconess Christine and her husband are responding to the violence in the area by living and working with the people

4. "Working alongside" translates to "*bayanihan*" in Tagalog. This is a highly valued aspect of Philippine culture.

5. Red-tagging is a common tactic in the Philippines. It means to label a person or place "communist" to justify killing with impunity.

directly affected. She told me that they have indigenous students at Greene Academy, and two of them have graduated and are now in college. It was obvious that she was both proud of this and that she found joy in it.

I found joy in what she told me! In 2017, on my first trip to the Philippines, my team leader, Joy, and I had embedded for a week in a school for indigenous children not too far from Greene Academy. My heart is still with those children. Education was so important to their parents that they had worked with churches and religious groups to build several schools to serve the indigenous tribes who had been denied an education. The school I had stayed at on that first trip was taken over by the military early in 2018 and has since been closed completely. I saw several of the students on "*bakwit*" (evacuation) in Manila later that year. Christine knew some of the same young people that I had met, including Jurain, who had become a victim of an extrajudicial killing. Without saying much about it, Deaconess Christine understood my feelings, and I understood hers. I am grateful for this level of closure. It allowed me to move from grief to joy, knowing that some of those students have found a way to continue the education that is very important to them. And I learned from Christine that being part of the education of those students is a powerful response to injustice, a way of resistance. And in the act of resisting injustice, there is the joy of knowing you are not helpless, and the situation is not hopeless.

I also love children. I taught school for ten years before attending seminary. I understand these deaconess/home missioners who followed their hearts to serve God and find joy through teaching. Like Deaconess Ruth and others, I miss being in the classroom. This might be part of the reason I wanted to get to know more deaconesses in the Philippines. I am grateful to know so many people with similar hearts. The relationships I began in April of 2023 with these women and the commonalities I found with them are a glimmer of what *kapwa* means.

I can connect with their stories of finding joy and realized that, like them, I find joy and fulfillment in doing what God calls me to do. Looking back, there were points of light for me in the darkness of pandemic restrictions. Preaching virtually was one. Beginning a DMin program and forming relationships within the cohort virtually was another. Weekly Zoom sessions with family and initiating and attending Zoom sessions between deaconess/home missioners in the US and the Philippines were very bright moments. All of this and more was eclipsed by the darkness of the pandemic at the time, but it is becoming real to me as I reflect on the joys that deaconess/home missioners told me about. There is always joy in doing God's work, and in the families that God has given us.

How Do You Find Hope?

> But Jacob stayed apart by himself, and a man wrestled with him until dawn broke. . . . The man said, "Let me go because the dawn is breaking." But Jacob said, "I won't let you go until you bless me." (Gen 32:24, 26)

> If you have faith, you will receive what you pray for. (Matt 21:22)

Bargaining, pleading, demanding, disappointment, frustration, anger. Bringing everything they're feeling and demanding what they need. Not reticent or afraid to lay it all out in front of God. Like Jacob, who did not stop wrestling with the "man" (God) until he was blessed, deaconess/home missioners do not pray weak and careful prayers but instead boldly say what is on their hearts. They have faith that they will receive it. As a result, they find hope during their prayer time. They trust God to act. If they don't trust God to answer when they begin to pray, they pray until they know God is with them.

"God, you called me to do this, now help me do it!" When I was interviewing Deaconess Hazel Sablay in Kabacan, Mindanao, she told me she has prayed this way many times. Unashamed, she admits to bargaining with God, demanding what she needs to be able to serve others. Others told me they pray like this—"We have no food in the house and my salary is not enough! We need your help!" And time after time, help arrives. They pray boldly. They pour out their hearts and all their feelings to God who is able to hold it all. And then their prayers are answered.

Here in the US, I have had a different experience of prayer. We tend to pray more cautiously, seeming to want to cover our bases if a prayer goes unanswered or is not answered the way we want it to be. "God, if it be your will, please do such and such" is a model for prayer here. We tend to hold back, even in desperate cases. We want to leave ourselves an open door, a way to say, "It must not have been God's will." As if unanswered prayer would make a desperate situation worse. As if we don't really believe God will answer our prayer. If that's true, then why are we praying?

Deaconess/home missioners in the Philippines go into their prayer time and close that escape door. They wrestle with God until their prayers are heard. They give it all to God and God blesses them, giving them what they need.

"Can I pray more like this?" I wondered. Am I confident enough to pray like these prayer warriors? Do I trust God enough to speak my mind and open my heart this way? I am learning to be more courageous and less wimpy in the way I pray. As a result, I am trusting God more and more. And I am sometimes (actually often!) overwhelmed because God takes care of me in ways that I don't even know to ask for. All because I am learning to pray the way deaconess/home missioners in the Philippines pray.

And it's an amazing thing! Because I see that prayers are answered, I have more hope that things will not stay as bad as they seem right now. I trust that God is intervening and will continue to be active in the world. Why do I believe this? Because the deaconess/home missioners in the Philippines so obviously believe it. If they don't, they wouldn't pray so demandingly, so strongly.

As I have studied more about Filipino theology, I learned something that might be at least part of the reason prayers are bolder in the Philippines. Early in the sixteenth century, in the early days of Spanish colonialism, there were a few missionaries who decided it was important to develop a culturally sensitive translation of the Lord's Prayer. They realized that for Christianity to be relevant to the indigenous peoples, they needed to use language that made sense to them, that fit into the way they lived and what was important to them—home and family, what food they ate, relationships, the philosophy of *kapwa* (the shared inner self, which is the strength found in togetherness in a communal society), and the concept of God's *loob*, which has been translated as "will" but more accurately means essence or inmost self, in other words, God's love. This is an English translation of part of what they came up with:

> Make Your Reign come home to us. Make Your whole, most authentic and relational Self be followed. Give us today rice to eat. Do not leave us so we are not overcome by temptation.[6]

It is much gentler to pray for God's reign to "come home to us" than to say "Thy Kingdom come," which can sound like a mandate from a stern God. Much friendlier to ask that people would follow God than "Thy will be done!" which, to my ears, sounds like an order to people rather than a prayer to God. And how sweet it is to pray to God not to leave us so that we will be safe from temptation. With this gentler, friendlier prayer, this kinder, more caring image of God, I can pray more boldly too! For God to say "I offer you my most authentic self so you can follow me" leaves space to approach God with less fear and more honesty. If, as a society, people could have this understanding of God, maybe they could pray more boldly. Maybe then it wouldn't be only the deaconess/home missioners in the Philippines.

How Do You Stay Committed When It's Challenging?

> As a result of all this, my loved brothers and sisters, you must stand firm, unshakable, excelling in the work of the

6. de Mesa, "Inculturation," 17

> Lord as always, because you know that your labor isn't going to be for nothing in the Lord. (1 Cor 15:58)

In the past, I have sometimes found my employment difficult, even nearly intolerable, but nothing I have experienced compares to the challenges many of the women and men I interviewed face on a regular basis. Meeting the needs of people living in extreme poverty, receiving less than a living wage, being appointed to a church far from their spouse, working so many hours per week that they are forced to neglect their own children are all incredibly challenging. And then there are times when the call for justice for the poor collides with government policies and, with the ever-present threat of being red-tagged (labeled a communist) by the government, makes me wonder how deaconess/home missioners are courageous enough to remain committed to their calling to love, justice, and service.

Commitment seems difficult to come by these days. Commitment to a vocation or a career seems to have fallen to the desire to make the highest salary. Commitment to relationships becomes difficult, so we walk away. Even commitment to family can fade. And commitment to God can be fragile and break when God does not match what we have come to believe. But for Philippine deaconess/home missioners, their faithful resolve is planted deep inside. Consecrated to love, justice, and service, they remain assured that God will always provide for their needs and answer their prayers and guide them as they serve. They are committed to their calling, which they understand, put broadly, to include sharing Christ with others, especially with the children of the church. This is the purpose of their ministry. It's why they became deaconess/home missioners. It's what their training focused on and where they find joy. Even though they could earn more money in the public schools, the majority of them honor their consecration, the lifetime commitment they made to serve God.

Deaconess Mimi (Karmina) Lopez, who serves at Puno UMC in Quezon City in the Metro Manila area, laughingly tells me that she sometimes finds it hard to get up in the morning, but she gets out of bed because she knows that "God will be active in this day."

For her, this is the grace of God, and it motivates her to get up, determined to join in the work that God is doing. "Every *gising* (wake-up) is a blessing" is a common saying in the Philippines, and it has become a part of Mimi's routine. It reminds her that each day is a gift from God to do God's work, and she is grateful for that. That gratitude is the source of her commitment.

Deaconess Michelle Dudang-Ortiz, who also serves in Puno UMC, remembers admiring the work ethic of the deaconesses she knew when she was young. "Morning, afternoon, until evening they are in the church. . . . And as a deaconess now, I give back to the Lord what he has done for me. . . . That is my service, my dedication as a deaconess, because I know this is his will for me to be a deaconess in the church. So I give all, even my time, my resources, toward the church." When I interviewed her in April of 2023, Michelle was working toward her master's degree in special education to be better equipped to respond to needs she sees in her classroom. She is committed to giving more back to God by becoming a better-equipped teacher for her students. She has since completed her degree.

Deaconess Helen Asuncion at Fairview Park UMC (also in Quezon City) told me that she was not willing, at first, to become a deaconess. Her father is a pastor, and when she was young, he was at church so much, she says, that he seemed to forget he had a family. "But then I personally realized that he just does it for the glory of the Lord, he loves the Lord, and through that I am very inspired. . . . Because of that, because of what I saw in my father's dedication in the ministry," she says, she was inspired to become a deaconess. She remains faithful and, like Michelle, she has answered God's call to better serve the needs of people with disabilities by earning her master's degree in special education.

Deaconess Lady Lhou Ganal at Obrero United Methodist Church in Davao City, Mindanao, describes her commitment this way: "The purpose of my ministry is to devote myself, my life, to serving the local churches in the ministry that God has entrusted to me and to use my God-given gifts to build one another in the faith and knowledge of the Lord God, especially in teaching the little children." She is, like many other deaconesses, married to the pastor and is his committed partner in ministry to the congregation they serve.

Deaconess Ruth Trube, who also serves in Davao City, previously served as a Christian educator and a kindergarten teacher in a church. When I interviewed her, she was appointed as the director of Davao United Methodist Mission Center, Inc., facilitating outreach and mission in this urban setting. She is committed to this way of being in ministry, seeing it not only as a way to serve the neighboring community, but also as a means of increasing her abilities and skills. Even though there are challenges that can sometimes be discouraging and disappointing, her conviction that "God is walking before me" has resulted in a strong commitment to the important work she is doing. The word "mission" often came up in our conversation. Her personal mission is to teach children to read, even the ones who have not learned by the age of ten or eleven. This is in addition to her appointed work at the Davao Mission Center, serving those living in poverty without permanent shelter. She gives her best efforts to find ways to get food to the hungry, and to provide religious instruction to people who might not ever go to church. It is also part of the program of the Mission Center to coordinate with local government agencies which are also serving the poor. This is not something that Ruth was trained for, but her desire to make all of this happen is evidence that her mission to children and to others living in poverty is very important to her. She, like others I interviewed, is effective in the ministry she is appointed to, even though it was not what she envisioned doing when she first thought of becoming a deaconess.

For a few deaconess/home missioners, the financial hardship is too much. Sometimes they are appointed to a place that requires living far from their spouse and even their children. They come to a decision to leave being a deaconess/home missioner, maybe temporarily or maybe permanently. It's a matter of self-care, of being able to care properly for themselves and their children. When I see their hearts, as Emma has taught me to do, I see that the commitment to God is still there. It just takes on a different form.

I have learned a lot about commitment from deaconess/home missioners. Working for a higher cause, leading children and others to Jesus, teaching children to read, feeding the hungry, and more, all of it comes from their deep gratitude for all that God does for them. Even when they struggle, they see God at work in their lives, not blaming God, but seeing God's grace and mercy. Their eyes can see the blessings in everything. I am learning to see them as well. As Deaconess Mimi says, "Every *gising* (wake-up) is a blessing." I have sometimes struggled to feel that way. My heart's prayer is that I may always see God's presence new every morning and feel blessed.

Interlude

Davao City

Facing east, watching the lights of the city come on,
I cannot see the sunset,
only those lights that shine in the increasing darkness.
They would not be possible without
the hands and feet and minds of humans.
The darkness would overcome the city lights
if the power grid fails
or if somehow all the bulbs burn out at once.
Still the lights shine.
The efforts of humans shine.
Shine, symbols of hope!
Despite hardship and struggle,
grief and loneliness,
hopelessness and despair,
these lights still shine!
Darkness falls,
but we, the humans, beat it back

with our own light.
The work we do matters!
The love we share matters!
The hope we find matters!
Each moment we work to move the world
closer to God's kin-dom
coming on earth as it is in heaven—
it all matters!

Mindanao

> John the Baptist was in the wilderness calling for people to be baptized to show that they were changing their hearts and lives and wanted God to forgive their sins. (Mark 1:4)

Mindanao. Huge plantations of banana, pineapple, rice, and sugar cane. The wide, flat rice fields. Orchards of mango, mangosteen, papaya, and many other kinds of fruit. Groves of palm for coconut and oil. Huts line the roadsides to sell what is harvested. Fresh pineapple pieces packaged in a plastic bag come with a fork so I can eat as we drive, juice dribbling down my chin. Unrefined sugar is sold in larger bags, tastes like candy right out of the bag, elevates the flavor of tea above anything tasted ever before. Tempting to buy it all, taste it all, gorge on fruit until one more bite is just not possible. The generosity of the black volcanic soil seems endless.

All this gives way to the mountains, the sources of that soil. Mt. Matutum, the little brother. Mt. Apo, the elder. Holy to the indigenous peoples. Home for them as well. The road winds through the range, giving glimpses of ocean, islands, the horizon. On the other side of the mountains is the coast. Reminiscent, in a more humid way, of some stretches of the Pacific Coast Highway in California. Flashes of sun reflected on the water between the trees, homes, and shops reveal the Gulf of Davao. Tantalizing and beautiful.

Poverty does not diminish the beauty here. It only adds to the awareness of the disparity between the wealth of the corporations that own the plantations and the needs of the people who live on Mindanao. The richness of the land does not enrich the people who live there. The systemic imbalance disturbs me. Motivates me. Perhaps this is part of what motivates the deaconess/home missioners here as well.

Interlude

A Prayer

Igpaw Mindanao![1]

Do not give your soul to the greed and grabbing of the outside world.

Do not let fear win!

"'The time will come,' says the Lord,

'when you will rise up on wings like eagles.'"[2]

Igpaw Mindanao!

Your spirit lives and your creator is with you!

Creation groans and you cry out!

The one who made the land and all that lives on it

has not abandoned the land or you.

1. "*Igpaw*" means "leap over" or "overcome." I first heard the phrase "*Igpaw* Mindanao" in a song sung by Lumad (indigenous) youth at a school that was built by donors to educate them. I heard the song again the next year in Metro Manila, sung by the same young people, then on *Bakwit* (evacuation) because the military had taken over their school.

2. After Isa 40:31.

Igpaw Mindanao!

Beautiful island.

Land of pineapple, sugar cane, rice, banana, mango, and so much more!

Land of warm smiles and strong earthquakes!

Strong men and determined women.

My heart longs to return to you.

May your people find peace and joy.

On my first trip to the Philippines in 2017, I spent six days on Mindanao, the southernmost island, close to the equator. It was under martial law then, and in 2023 the vestiges of that time remained. Maybe they are permanent. Checkpoints along the highway, mostly un-staffed now, are still barriers that slow vehicles. Occasionally one is still in use to look for criminals or something else. I was nervous, at first, about returning, but Emma wanted to bring me there, so I went. Emma was always with me, my guide and assurance. Pastor Lyndon Castillo served as our driver, and his wife, Deaconess Janice Arcibal Castillo, and their two beautiful children accompanied us. Lyndon's mother, Deaconess Emelyn Castillo, was our guide. Having so many people with me, especially two young ones, helped me relax and enjoy this adventure.

I interviewed fourteen people in Mindanao, two in Davao City and the rest in the Cotabato region to the southwest of Davao. All but one of them had been educated at the Southern Philippines Methodist Colleges, Inc. (SPMCI). This area is different from the Metro Manila area.

At the Vacation Bible School training in Kabacan. Including Home Missioner Joel Gacote, left, Deaconess Adeline Cornito, middle, in green, and Deaconess Hazel Sablay, in checked pants. Deaconess Lady Lhou Ganal, far right, was interviewed in Davao City.

It is rural, agricultural. The deaconess/home missioners are more adapted to doing their work without another deaconess/home missioner nearby. Some are serving as church pastors because there is a shortage of clergy. There seems to be less confidence in speaking English for some, and I was grateful for Emma's help with translation a few times. The people speak Bisayan, which is different from Tagalog, and less familiar to me. One thing I noticed is that when they called me "ma'am," the pronunciation is broader, more like "mom," while in the north, it is shorter, closer to "mam." In addition, the churches in the countryside are more spread out than in the city, and smaller. Deaconess/home missioners have to travel further to meet together. I interviewed seven deaconess/home missioners at a Vacation Church School[3] training event in Kabacan (pronounced Kah-BOCK-an). It would

3. Vacation Church School is a traditional annual United Methodist event. Children are taught Bible stories and songs in a fun and engaging way. In the Philippines, it is led by deaconess/home missioners.

not have been easy to visit all their churches. At the end of the day, we took home a few of the people who lived not too far outside of town. It would have been a long walk and it was late in the day. I was glad to see where people lived and served.

The challenges of ministry in Mindanao came up in interviews and other conversations. They include isolation, difficult transportation, limited internet in many places, and long work-weeks with only rare days off. Working long hours too often means sacrificing time with their own families. Harassment and lack of respect for their important work is a problem for some. Strong earthquakes (over 6.0) are common, damaging buildings and homes and sometimes killing people. There are also typhoons, landslides, floods, and other natural disasters to survive and recover from. From the deaconess/home missioners there, I learned that being faithful to God's call is sometimes a prayer repeated for strength and persistence.

Two of the people I interviewed in Kabacan were home missioners. While I had heard that young men in the Philippines were beginning to hear God calling them to be home missioners, this was the first time that I had the opportunity to meet any of them. Home missioners Joel Gacote and Romelito Gallardo could not have been any more different. Joel bounced into the interview with great excitement and began speaking before I could even introduce myself. He was the only interviewee in Mindanao who called me "Sharon" instead of "ma'am" or "Miss Sharon." A very confident, extroverted young man. In contrast, Romelito came in quietly and admitted to being very nervous. He spoke so softly that I had to lean forward to hear him. They were the first two home missioners to be consecrated in Mindanao. They, like all but one of the deaconesses there, were graduates of Southern Philippines Methodist Colleges, Inc. (SPMCI). They were both commissioned in 2022. They have interesting and very different call stories.

When asked why he chose to be a home missioner instead of clergy, Joel said that he had started as a candidate for ministry, but no one encouraged him or gave him books to read to learn more about it. He told me that when he went to SPMCI (which has a program for clergy candidates as well as for deaconess/home missioners), the "scholarship available is not for theology, but for deaconess service, so because I wanted to pursue my college, I enroll. I take the challenge." After graduation, he decided to apply to be consecrated as a home missioner. Many people tried to discourage him because there were no home missioners yet, but he decided he wanted to be the first one! He also told me that he had hated music class all through his younger years, that he skipped class all the time. However, when he was sixteen years old, God called him to help his pastor, so he taught himself how to play piano by painting a keyboard on plywood, then holding a book in his left hand and touching the "keys" with his right, imagining how it would sound. He was only able to practice on a real keyboard in church on Sundays. And now he loves music, conducting the choir, teaching the children. It shows in the way he lights up when he talks about all of this. This is one of the most dramatic call stories I have heard. I think it is rare that a person changes from hating something to loving it the way Joel does.

Romelito told me a more difficult story. In high school, he experienced a tragedy in which "there was a bottle of liquor, and it broke and someone got cut." Without giving any more details about that, he admitted that he had the vices (as he called them) of drinking and smoking. His aunt, a deaconess, encouraged him to come to the church where she was appointed. She learned that he was "good in music, particularly in piano." She became determined that he would go to college. He was still drinking and smoking when he began studying, but he quit both when "I accepted God in my heart and in my soul. I'm asking God if it is my calling. . . . God answered those questions in my mind, so that is why I decided to be a home missioner." Just as I had asked Joel, I asked him why home missioner and not clergy. His decision was not firm. His aunt told him that he could change his mind later if he wanted to. I believe that his aunt was a good role model who did a lot to help him, so he wanted to become a church worker like her.

From these two home missioners, I learned that God can change your life for the better.

6

Attending Events

> Jesus said, "I'm no longer in the world, but they are in the world, even as I'm coming to you. Holy Father, watch over them in your name, the name you gave me, that they will be one just as we are one." (John 17:11)

Diakonia Asia Pacific

IN THE FALL OF 2023, the first item on my itinerary was to travel to Tagaytay, about a two-hour drive south of Manila, for a meeting of Diakonia Asia Pacific (DAP). DAP is an ecumenical organization of deaconesses and deacons from Southeast Asia and the South Pacific. I had just arrived in Manila the evening before, but my excitement overcame my need for sleep, at least for a few hours. I was very happy to ride with Jennifer Ferariza Meneses, executive secretary of the Board of Women's Work in the United Methodist Philippines Regional Conference, and Deaconess Bless de Leon, both friends from prior trips.

As we drove, the urban area gave way to the suburbs and new development, then to a more rural setting. As that happened, the road changed from tollway to highway, narrowing down to two lanes. I smiled as we passed a sign for a "Waltermart Store," and again when we saw goats grazing by the side of the road. It felt something like home while at the same time somehow being completely different from where I live in coastal Southern California.

We turned onto narrower and narrower roads and finally into a gated gravel driveway, then parked in front of a beautiful building surrounded by flowers and lush greenery. As we went around the side of the building, we were welcomed by the sound of women singing in harmony.

The women were worshiping at the beginning of their time together. What beautiful music, the women blending their voices, giving glory to God! We walked in and found places to sit, mixing with the ecumenical group. Ruby-Nell Estrella, the first female United Methodist bishop in the Philippines, brought us a "Message of Life," in which she told us that justice means "right relationship with creation and with humanity." Deaconess Chita Framo, former president of DAP, also spoke. She was followed by the Rev. Glofie Gonzales Baluntong, who began by telling us that, after serving as a deaconess for twenty-four years, she decided to become an ordained clergyperson.

Retired Deaconess Chita Framo speaks to the group.

Then, in 2021, because she was following Christ's mandate to feed the poor, she was arrested on false charges of "frustrated murder" (that is, attempted murder). She was finally cleared of charges in December 2025, over two years after I heard her speaking at DAP. Prior to her arrest, military personnel were harassing and intimidating her. She was red-tagged, which put her life in constant danger. At any time, she could have become the victim of an extrajudicial killing, as have far too many others. Even if a semblance of an investigation is conducted into such killings, a suspect is never arrested in cases. No justice results. In her talk, she admitted to being afraid for her life, yet she continued to minister, to speak out against injustice, and to speak at events, being open and vulnerable in a way I have never had to consider for myself. Her words challenged as well as inspired me. I put my personal safety as a high priority most of the time, and when meeting this kind of courage, I feel at least somewhat ashamed. I am reminded of Deaconess Doring Bravo, who ministered under the noses of the occupying Japanese forces in World War II. Deaconesses have courage. What kind of courage do I have? I still don't know.

I was sitting with women from the United Church of Christ Philippines (UCCP),[1] so I wasn't even interacting with United Methodists much that morning. It seemed to me that was the purpose of attending an ecumenical gathering. I also spoke to a delegate from Fiji and the Diakonia Asia Pacific president, Australian Sandy Boyce. I enjoyed every minute of this relationship-building time, stretching out beyond United Methodism to connect with other women who serve God. Despite being from outside the Asia Pacific region (I am a member of Diakonia of the Americas and the Caribbean), I was welcomed warmly. I was asked to bring greetings from the deaconess/home missioners in the US, and I was invited to be part of the picture-taking at the

1. The United Church of Christ Philippines (UCCP) is distinct from the United Church of Christ that we know in the United States. It was formed in the Philippines in 1948 by the union of several denominations: Presbyterian, Philippine Methodist, Brethren, Disciples, and Congregational. See the bibliography for the url for United Church of Christ in the Philippines, "About Us."

end of the morning. Lunch together was a time of conversation and getting to know each other.

After we ate, jet lag hit me on the head. It was time to go back to the Metro Manila area, to Quezon City, to Decker Home for Retired Deaconesses, my "home away from home" in the Philippines, to rest and get adjusted to the time difference.

Interlude

Rainstorm!

There is nothing
like a Philippine rainstorm.
The humidity all gangs up and falls
suddenly
out of the sky,
announcing itself as
loudly as it can when it
hits
the metal roof!

Santiago City, Isabela with "A Women"

At 4 a.m. on a Wednesday, I waited outside in the dark under the wide covered patio at Decker House. Soon, Pastor Sandy Khemlani came out to join me. A car came to pick us up. We had time to get acquainted. Although she lives at Decker House where I was staying, until this day we had seen each other only in passing, exchanging quick hellos. We were about to get better acquainted.

Pastor Sandy is the assistant to Bishop Ruby-Nell Estrella, the first woman bishop in the United Methodist Central Conference. Competent and intelligent, with an attitude that likely answers criticism with a smirk, she also has a sense of humor. This personality combination seems to me to be very useful in her position.

We were headed to a two-day leadership training event for A Women in Santiago City, Isabela. A Women ("A" for "active") is a group of young women who serve as ordained ministers, deaconesses, and lay ministers in the Central Luzon Annual Conference. I rarely get to spend time with young women, and I was excited to learn with them and from them, as well as getting to know them.

We stopped to pick up the rest of the leadership team on the way—Jenn Meneses, Deaconess Bless de Leon, Global Mission Fellow Srey Non Bo, and Deaconess April Grace Martinez. Deaconess Sheena Calma and Rev. Rhen Mungcal joined us when we stopped for breakfast in Pampanga. To fit everyone in, at that point we exchanged the sedan for a van for the rest of the trip.

We headed north and then east, over the Cordillera Mountains. The road was steep and winding, with many hairpin turns. There were several places where rockslides had closed one side of the road. Fortunately, people slowed down to let the other side pass. There were many motorcycles on this route, and I worried one would hit a patch of gravel and go down. I was even more concerned as we neared the summit and the wind picked up. And then it started raining. I said a prayer for safe travels for everyone on the road. Soon enough, we were on our way down the other side and not long after that, the road began to straighten out, headed toward Santiago City in the valley.

We passed through the town of Cordon and were slowed by a crowd of pedestrians, trikes (motorcycles with sidecars for hire), and motorcycles. It was All Saints' Day, when it is the tradition to visit the graves of loved ones. The cemetery was alongside the highway. Vendors were selling flowers and other items. People looked for a place to park. People walked across the street without regard for traffic. We went slowly, cautiously, and soon we were back on the open road, heading toward our destination. We arrived at about 4 p.m., twelve hours after I was waiting in the dark at Decker. A long, long day. We had made it safely. The next morning people arrived at the conference center, excited to be together. I settled in, ready to see what the day would bring. Every gathering begins with worship, lovely voices singing beautiful songs together, prayer, a sermon about a couple in Scripture named Priscilla and Aquila (the wife is named first because she is more prominent in the church)—to set the tone for the meeting.

A wooden sculpture of a woman holding a baby over her head, kissing her.

The altar was very beautiful. It included a wooden sculpture made of reddish wood showing a kneeling woman with her hair tied back, holding a baby up over her head, kissing her. Including such a feminine piece of artwork on an altar had a great impact on me. It emphasized what is sometimes downplayed, that women are loved by God, that what is important to women is holy and sacred, and that what we bring to God's table is love, nurture, and strength. In addition, it points out that God, being spirit, also has a feminine aspect that is often disregarded.

This event was entitled "Women's Spirituality and Development: A Leadership Formation Program of the A Women," a program of the Board of Women's Work, which is the Philippine branch of United Women in Faith. Sessions included background about the realities that women experience today and a call to action in response, information about systemic gender oppression, an introduction to feminist theology, and how to read Scripture from a woman's point of view. Although I have been a feminist for at least half a century, I found all this interesting and illuminating. To hear it all from young women put a twenty-first-century point on it for me.

I also enjoyed relearning the One Billion Rising dance. I learned it several years before but had forgotten much of it. Some of the steps and arm movements reflect self-defense moves such as pushing away and punching out, while others celebrate women's power in other ways. It acts out a powerful message of ending violence against women and children in a way that feels empowering, and dancing together brings a strength and a physicality to solidarity and resistance.

I was honored and humbled to lead the devotion on the second morning. I drew it from Matt 24:36. My topic was solidarity and the desire of Christ for all of us to be one, "even as we [the Holy Trinity] are one." It fit the theme of the meeting. (The complete text of this devotion can be found in appendix II.)

The schedule for this two-day event was so busy that finding time to interview was difficult, but Deaconess April Grace Martinez and I found half an hour during a lunch break. Grace (as she asked me to call her) is one of the members of the leadership team for A Women. When we went to a mall for dinner one evening, I saw her walking and talking with Deaconess Bless de Leon. Bless is a mentor to many, I think. Perhaps that includes Grace. There is a great emphasis on leadership development in the Philippines, bringing younger people into positions where they can learn and grow from those who are more experienced so they will be prepared for taking on more and more responsibility with time. This works well, and there are people of all ages working in United Methodist Headquarters and in other offices and organizations. This diversity in age blends experience and proven ideas with energy and creativity, producing great results that I have witnessed in every event I have attended in the Philippines.

Grace is a young, energetic deaconess whose laugh comes easily and sounds like bells ringing. When I interviewed her, she was on study leave, earning her master's degree in education, which she finished in May 2024. She already had over seven years' experience in teaching kindergarten. She also is a Christian educator and has worked as an advisor for youth, guiding them and sharing Christ with them. She has a gift for helping them know that they are not going through their struggles alone. During the pandemic, she found a way to help them when they needed fellowship. The lockdown in the Philippines was strict. She told me that "when we cannot go outside, communication started. My Messenger [online private messaging] was busy." When the restrictions lifted a little, "the youth came to me saying, 'We truly miss each other. We miss the fellowship. We miss learning about God.' We started with a minimum protocol." Grace was careful, still, and when there were no COVID cases in the area, she organized activities, starting with ten participants, then growing the group to forty-five. She had to get approval for this not only from the church council but from the municipality, because health restrictions were still in effect. She told me, with a bit of awe in her voice, "Because of their love to have fellowship, I made all things possible through Christ, and we are liable if there would be COVID cases, but thank God, there's no young people who got COVID, despite all the activities that we did! So, the pandemic was—*fun*? For me, somehow? I am not thanking God for COVID, no, I am not!" She laughed and shook her head as she said that, but she was grateful to God for helping her and the young people find a way to meet together while still staying well. Not all these young people belonged to The United Methodist Church, and this was an opportunity for her to share the love of Christ with all of them, Methodist or not. "We created a community that accepted, that takes care of their mental health and help them get through their anxious experiences, especially when they were alone at home." This is the best pandemic story I have heard from anyone. It impresses me and inspires me.

Grace also told me about a young girl who attended the group with a friend. She was being molested by her father. When she was removed from her home by social services, she was able to stay with a member of the youth group, and the church became a safe place for her. Grace told me, "She was nurtured in the church. Instead of pulling herself from God, she let God move in her life. And I've seen her grow in her leadership at school and at church. That experience did not let her go down in life, just as one who will cry and so on." Instead, Grace told me, she is a leader in the group, bringing others to church, because she found young people there who stand beside her, who listen to her and support her. From Grace I learned that God is able to bring good out of the worst circumstances, and that people who support and listen to others are a source of healing and strength. This is church at its best.

On the third day we headed home. We made a couple of stops as we went back over the Cordillera Mountains, one at the Mapico Viewpoint, where we could look down the beautiful canyon, and a second at a roadside vegetable stand owned by indigenous people. I bought some delicious tomatoes.

The rugged Cordillera Mountains.

Later, we stopped in a town named Mexico, where each fall they have a shopping area very beautifully decorated for Christmas. We enjoyed the lights and huge versions of the Christmas star lanterns called *parol.* There was also a spectacular dry lightning storm happening nearby, with cloud-to-cloud lightning. A God-made light show as a backdrop to a human-made light show.

It was very late when we got home, so I needed a day of rest on Sunday. Monday and Tuesday were also stay-at-home days for resting and preparing a devotional and two presentations I would make later in the week. By this time, I was more used to the heat and humidity and could sit outside to write. Decker House is a beautiful place, and it was good to be outside to enjoy it. People and pets wander by, providing pleasant distractions, but not so much that work failed to get done. A perfect place to write.

Interlude

Writing a Devotion

I sat down to write, my feet propped on a chair.

It was hot and humid and I didn't know what to say.

What could I write a devotion about?

Something about disability or mental illness was requested.

I studied the gigantic mango tree that shades the driveway
and the front garden.

I wondered if I could grow flowers like the ones
edging the garden.

I heard dogs barking. The orange cat wandered past.

And then, I think I stopped thinking!

My hands moved and I typed, "The man living in the cemetery."

We had passed a cemetery on our trip north on All Saints' Day.

Had that sparked an idea?

Jesus went to the man where he lived in the cemetery.

He could have taken himself to the wilderness,
to an isolated place.

But he was in the cemetery. He had found a home
among the dead.

A place for my thoughts to start . . .

United Methodist Headquarters

I had been asked to lead a devotion for the staff at United Methodist Church Headquarters in addition to the one at the A Women Leadership Training event, so I had brought two already-prepared messages from home. Once I was there, however, neither seemed appropriate for either presentation, so I wrote new ones. For the Disability Ministries and Mental Health Consultation, I was asked for something that would raise awareness among the conference staff of the importance of the Consultation. I sat at a table in the covered patio, ready to write. My thoughts meandered for a bit until they landed on the story of the man possessed by a legion of demons.

In the past, I have considered this story difficult to preach. At first glance, demon possession doesn't seem particularly salient today in our post-Enlightenment, postmodern era. But as I pondered what to write, I realized that this story of a man living among the dead in a graveyard, clearly mentally ill, is very relevant to us. Jesus came to him. When the man saw Jesus, he ran and knelt down in front of him, begging Jesus not to torture him. He had been howling and cutting himself. Maybe he was having suicidal thoughts and Jesus came to save him from himself. By looking at this passage from the point of view of the ill man, I found it easy to prepare a message.[1]

When I shared it with the headquarters staff, the responses included a listing of the children of clergy and deaconesses who had died recently by their own hands. Clearly the consultation on

1. An edited version of this message is in the appendix.

mental health was badly needed. I was asked to share this same devotion during the consultation.

Changing my point of view is a practice I learned in the Philippines through conversations with deaconesses and others. In a country where so many live in poverty, with a large percentage struggling with extreme poverty, it is often in-your-face clear that if an interpretation is not good news for the poor, it is not the gospel of Jesus Christ. And just because the language used in Scripture isn't the way we talk about certain things doesn't mean the message is not relevant to us. I am still learning to turn stories around to find the way that the poor would understand them, the way that the people of Jesus' day understood them. I learned something important from Dr. Revelation Velunta—that the master/king figure does not always or even usually represent God. I first met the professor at Union Theological Seminary in Cavite, south of Manila, where I first heard this new-to-me interpretation of the Scriptures. I reach for his book, *Reading the Parables of Jesus Inside a Jeepney*,[2] whenever I need to readjust my Western/European mindset and continue working toward this paradigm shift to interpret Scripture through the lens of another culture, a different economic status, the experiences of people different from us. I am attempting to step out of the boots of the colonizer into the sandals of the colonized. This takes work, but it's worth it.

Deaconess Darlene Marquez Caramanzana

The next interview helped me to better put this transformation into words. I sat down with Deaconess Darlene Marquez Caramanzana, liaison to the United Methodist General Board of Global Missions in their Asia Pacific office. This agency is the United Methodist source of humanitarian aid in response to disasters through its division, the United Methodist Committee on Relief (UMCOR), as well as its role in training and deploying missionaries around the world.

2. See the bibliography for more details. In addition, Professor Velunta has written several more books reinterpreting Scripture from the perspective of the poor.

Darlene is responsible for work being done in congregational development in the Philippines, Nepal, Myanmar, Indonesia, and part of Japan. She is also in charge of congregational work being done in India and Bangladesh, and she assists in leadership development training in Cambodia, Laos, and Vietnam, which are countries recently added to Global Missions. I was very curious about her work and grateful for this time to ask more about it.

Darlene and I had met in 2017 at NCCP on my first trip to the Philippines, and we had been together several times at various events. She is a petite woman with short brown hair and brown eyes, which are surrounded by stylish glasses. She always dresses very professionally. Her face is very open, her smile warm and frequent. Working for a General Board (that is, at the denominational level) is an unusual ministry for deaconess/home missioners in the Philippines. She is the only one I interviewed other than Emma Cantor who holds this kind of denominational position, though there are others.

When I asked her what gives her joy, Darlene talked first about her family. Both her husband and her son support her in her work, even though it requires her to travel often. Then she broadened her answer, saying that she finds joy in connecting with other people. She summarized deaconess/home missioner work this way: "I think at the heart of deaconess ministry is connection with people. We connect people, we connect communities. . . . This has always been an essential part of my ministry." In every way she has served—in the local church, at the National Council of Churches Philippines, on the Board of Women's Work, and now on the United Methodist General Board of Global Ministries—she has found connection to be a crucial part of her work. She emphasized that she could not thrive without it. Connection turned out to be the theme of this interview.

In the Philippines, deaconess/home missioners usually serve as Christian educators (in a church) or early childhood teachers (in a church-connected school). Many serve as both. Any appointment outside a local church is considered a special appointment. Darlene told me:

> Sometimes the tendency is to box the deaconess ministry into the church. . . . Somehow this is very limiting in terms of the depth and breadth of the deaconess ministry because, in truth, the deaconess ministry has always gone beyond the four walls of the church and has served communities. Communities of poor children, poor young people, poor women . . . and many other vulnerable communities.

She believes that deaconess/home missioners can be very influential in helping these communities realize their potentials and give them hope for a better future, and she can envision that bishops appointing deaconess/home missioners to a wider range of ministries would allow for more ways lives could be impacted.

She asserts that mission is also too often put into a box, with an outdated, colonial-era definition. She talked at length about what mission is today and how important it is for the future of The United Methodist Church. I agree, and I am glad that mission in The United Methodist Church has been moving away from colonialism and toward missionaries from many countries, not only from the United States.

One question I had been wrestling with had to do with the future of The United Methodist Church. For too many years the focus of our General Conferences[3] has been increasingly narrowed to differences in the understanding of Scripture about including or excluding people in the LGBTQI+[4] community. As I was writing this book, many congregations were disaffiliating, that is, leaving the denomination, with some forming a new denomination and others becoming independent. Would a smaller United Methodist denomination be weakened, less effective? What would happen to this denomination I loved so much? That so many of us grew up in, that taught us about Jesus and God? Would it, could it, survive?

3. The governing body of The United Methodist Church is General Conference. Meetings are held every four years to conduct the business of the worldwide denomination.

4. A commonly used acronym for lesbian, gay, bisexual, transgender, queer, intersex, and other nonheterosexual, non-cisgendered ("non-straight") people.

What Darlene told me about mission during this interview gave me hope by opening my eyes to the way forward.

Darlene shared that Global Missions in the Philippines had started a new program in 2022 to teach young people about mission. There are numerous young people and there is a very active UMYF (United Methodist Youth Fellowship) nationwide, yet very few of them know much about what mission is all about. Darlene and her coworkers saw this as an opportunity, so they began holding a regular School of Mission to teach them what mission is. She shared two stories about two young people who attended this program.

The first story was about a young man studying for his bachelor's degree in theology. His School of Mission group visited Union Theological Seminary (UTS) in Cavite, south of Manila, and the seminary took them to visit a nearby farming community. The farmers were fighting to retain their land against a private individual who claimed ownership. Their farms were the only way they had to feed their families. The students were welcomed into the farmers' homes. They played with the children. They heard their stories, felt their need to retain their land. They began relationships within the community. By the end of this program, the young student had decided to attend UTS. He is now working toward a master of divinity degree and has decided to become a pastor. Darlene says he realized that

> ministry is wide, that the ministry is really going beyond the four corners of the church and going to communities, engaging with people, listening to their stories, embracing their passion, embracing their struggles, and seeing their hope, that despite their struggles, despite harassment, despite getting pushed away from the land, they are still there.

This excited him by helping him to see the possibility of making a difference in the world by being a pastor in mission to serving the community. This definition of mission helped him hear his call to ministry.

The second story is similar, about a young man who was in leadership in the youth organization. He was in a different group of the School of Mission, also visiting UTS and going to the farming community. That group had been able to join the farmers in planting their crops. This young man became the communications coordinator for them, relaying news from the farmers to the group. One message informed them that the seeds they had planted were growing and a subsequent message let them know that there had been a successful harvest. In Darlene's words, they had learned how to "connect in community" and they had "learned the truthfulness in the relationships" they had built. She believes that learning there is more than one way of doing mission and knowing that mission is about relationship and connection will have an impact on the way they live and serve God in community in the future.

I call this definition of mission solidarity. Living in solidarity is leaving any semblance of colonialism or superiority behind and being in an equal, mutual relationship with people who are different from you, learning from each other and caring about each other's struggles and challenges as if they are your own. While I was learning about this School of Missions from Darlene, I felt her excitement as my own, and I wondered how such a program could be implemented in the US. Maybe it is a way to help young people see the value, the purpose, of church again, instead of turning away from church as being judgmental, hypocritical, and worthless. Maybe this broader understanding of mission as building connections and relationships would help people (young and old) find ways to make a difference in the world. In a spark of insight, I suddenly realized that this is a significant piece of why I have such a longing to continue to travel to the Philippines. The connections and the relationships I have developed there enable me to feel that I am not alone, and that together we are making this world a better place, simply by being there for each other and sharing our love and our light with each other.

Darlene continued, saying how we have "boxed mission" for too long by saying that mission is evangelism and/or helping others by building structures and feeding the hungry and not much else. We had a lengthy conversation then about my work as mission, that the solidarity and the connections that I make and the time that I spend listening to the stories of women is mission work. She stated, "It's also a mission of how you are bringing the voices of women to other places so that it's an inspiration." I have always called my project to write this book a mission. I expand the solidarity I feel with the people of the Philippines on every trip, understanding the culture better, knowing more about the way they think, the ways they live. It is not a mission that includes converting and saving others or repairing homes. Instead, it is a mission that is saving me from hopelessness and stagnation, freeing me to know more about what is truly important, and I hope it is also a mission to save deaconess/home missioners from being mostly unknown outside of the Philippines, raising them up to be role models. Solidarity and connection, in the way Darlene talks about them, are crucial in this world. Traveling can "take off the blinders," as Darlene says, and help us look away from the mirror in which we see only ourselves and instead really see others closer to the way God sees them. I believe that as we grow in solidarity and connection with others, we are working toward what has been called "the kingdom of God." I prefer the phrase "kin-dom of God" since it brings in the concept of being the family of God. I cannot understand how to build that kin-dom of God in any other way other than through relationships and solidarity. I don't see it as a shining city on a hill or some updated version of the garden of Eden. I see it as people everywhere understanding that we are all connected, each one aware of the joys and sorrows of each other, wanting the same for everyone else as we want for ourselves. Mission needs to be different now. We are no longer in the colonial era and we should let go of the attitude of the colonizers who believed that their mission was to civilize and save the heathen of other countries from eternal damnation. Instead, we need to understand that together, we can save each other, not through force and coerced baptism by those more powerful, but through mutual understanding and sharing and caring. This, ultimately, is what this book is about—that everything I have learned from deaconess/home missioners and others in the Philippines has led to solidarity, to connection and relationship, and all of this has saved me from despair and fear, depression and anxiety, feelings of being different and inadequate. I am grateful, not only to all the people I have met, especially those I have interviewed, but to God who called me to this work.

Deaconess Phebe Gamatta Crismo

After Darlene and I were finished, I went upstairs to the Office of the Board of Discipleship and Christian Education to meet with Deaconess Phebe Gamatta Crismo. She led me to her desk around display racks filled with books for Sunday school and Bible studies and through piles of quarterly magazines and books and other resources. "There is no warehouse," she explained. The only storage space is in her office. It seemed to me that everything must get moved out to churches and other places very quickly after publication or Phebe would soon be trapped behind all of it.

I had been introduced to Deaconess Phebe at least twice during my previous trips, but we had never spent any time together before sitting down for this interview. She is a great storyteller, a gift which makes her well suited to this position of writing and editing curricula, Bible studies, magazines of daily devotions, and much more. She came of age during martial law under Ferdinand Marcos, a time not only of huge disparity between rich and poor (maybe some of you remember Marcos' wife, Imelda, and her thousands of shoes?), but of terrible oppression. Phebe told me that she "wanted to live out [her] faith authentically, and in those days, you want to be a faithful Christian, you have to say 'no' . . . to military atrocities, to corruption, to human rights violations, and so forth and so on. Totalitarian rule." When she was a leader in the Methodist Youth Fellowship and the student movement, those groups were called "activists" and even "communists." Today this kind of red-tagging continues, putting anyone who stands up to corruption at risk of being the victim of extrajudicial killings. But Phebe is an activist in another way now, providing materials that teach others what it means to be authentic Christians, leading them to make their own decisions about what that looks like.

This boldness and activism led to her being expelled from Harris Memorial College after her third year. She had traveled with a group of young people to Hong Kong to participate in a Christian conference. Because she was interested in the arts as well as activism, she chose to be in a class that was performing a play about martial law. She believed it was her calling as a Christian, as a deaconess, so she stayed to perform after the conference was over. Because she missed her required summer fieldwork, the leadership at Harris notified her that she would no longer be enrolled. However, she had notified the bishop before spending her summer this way, so he helped her get reinstated. It would not be the last time that she was "kicked out" of being a deaconess for a transgression related to activism.

The second time came after she was married. After graduating from Harris Memorial College, Phebe was among the first batch of deaconesses to challenge the prohibition against marriage, but breaking that rule was not why she got in trouble. She married Romeo G. Crismo in July 1980. He was an activist working against the Marcos regime. Only sixteen days into their marriage, he was abducted by the military. Phebe searched for him without success. Soon she found herself guarded continuously by military personnel, ostensibly to keep her safe. She could not go anywhere or do anything without their knowledge. She went to her district superintendent (her supervisor) and informed him about this. Fearing for her safety, he told her to leave the province where everyone knew her and go to Manila. In the city, she would have the protection of anonymity. She was not able, then, to attend the annual meeting of her conference back in the province, a requirement for deaconesses and clergy. Without regard for her circumstances, she was removed as a deaconess. Since leaving her assignment was in response to the superintendent's order, she was later reinstated as a deaconess, but she remained in Manila. Away from family and friends, she faced additional challenges. It was only by God's grace that she found work and retained her mental health. She worked for a number of years at NCCP (National Council of Churches Philippines) in different positions that prepared her well for the highly demanding position of being the head of an agency of the Regional Conference.

As she told me all of this, I was impressed by her integrity and courage. When our planned disability consultation was going over budget because there was more interest than anticipated, she was the one to have the courage to ask the three bishops in the Philippines to make donations to bring the budget into the black. When a document was prepared for the resultant conference program addressing disabilities, she was the one with the knowledge and integrity to check it to ensure it was compliant with United Methodist doctrine. Because she is skilled and driven by her deep faith in the God who has brought her through so much hardship, people depend on her to handle many kinds of tasks, producing boxes and piles of educational and informative materials that are used by many others, primarily every deaconess/home missioner appointed to a church, to make disciples of all ages. The God she believes in is worthy of her best work.

Disability Consultation

The second national disability consultation in 2023 was planned for forty participants. Sixty had registered. That amount of interest was exciting. People arrived slowly, coming from many locations. They represented three Regional Conference entities—the Board of Women's Work, the Board of Church and Society, and the Board of Communication/Discipleship. This was historic, the first time that these three agencies had come together to plan a nationwide program to address a need!

As people arrived, the noise increased, punctuated by happy shouts as friends saw each other for the first time in a long time. I was excited, too, as I recognized people I knew from earlier trips and others that I had previously known only on social media.

The first day an overview of disabilities was presented. On the second day mental illness was covered. Experts came to teach.

People with disabilities added their expertise. Group discussions were lively and productive, even after dinner, when our time together approached twelve hours for the second day in a row. The best was saved for day three, when the representatives from each board met together to plan next steps. The end product was an initiative that will turn all the learning, all the thinking into action. It is inspiring to know that follow-up activities will move this new program forward to better serve and include people with disabilities and mental illness in the congregations of the Philippines Regional Conference.

A class of second-year student deaconess/home missioners came on a bus from Harris Memorial College. I asked their teacher, Dr. Zarla Raguindin, to choose one for me to interview, and soon Aliah Dizon and I were sitting together, and she was telling me her story. There was no quiet place available, but we managed to focus on each other for the most part, connecting with each other from different generations and cultures through our common love of Jesus Christ, children, and the church. Like many others I interviewed, Aliah shared her call story. As a girl, she had found a small United Methodist mission church in her area and was welcomed in, even as she continued to attend the Roman Catholic church her family attended. When she was twelve, she was invited to Christmas Institute, an annual gathering planned and led by deaconesses to help young people understand what it means to serve God. It includes an altar call, inviting people to come forward and dedicate their lives to Christ. She recounted her story this way: "I was just closing my eyes and I found out that I am in front, but I didn't feel that I'm walking, going to the front. Then I feel that someone is praying for me, and someone asked me my name . . . and they are asking me why do I want to be a deaconess." She was very confused. She had not walked forward. She had only closed her eyes. She had her own plan to become an architect, so she said she did not want to be a deaconess.

However, God had a different plan for her and was already preparing her to be a deaconess. She had already become a Sunday school teacher and gradually she found her patience with children growing and her ability to handle problems improving.

With deaconess-in-training, Aliah Broqueza Dizon, at the Disability/Mental Health Consultation.

Slowly she realized that God had called her when she first came to the mission church, so she prepared to enter Harris Memorial College to become a deaconess. It was still during the pandemic. In addition, her family could not afford the tuition. Both of those factors made it hard for her to decide to go. She prayed a bold prayer, saying, "Lord, if you have any plan for me to go to Harris, will you provide for all of my needs?" And God did, with a scholarship and sponsors and even an allowance. And she is very happy to go to Harris, choosing to follow God's plan instead of her own. Now in her second year, her confidence is increasing, and she appreciates all of her classes and teachers. Even the requirement to learn to play the piano, which was difficult for her, has become a source of comfort and fulfillment, a source of rest for her when she is tired. God has given her the gift of working alongside her in the struggle.

We spoke a bit about the quality of education at Harris, how she hears from friends at other universities that her classes are more advanced and how all her teachers are very good. She sounds very grateful and sure that she has made the right decision to become a deaconess.

At the end of this impactful three-day event, I was overwhelmed by God's grace and provision. I nearly fell to my knees, thinking about how all of this had started when I met Jenn Ferariza Meneses for the first time in 2017. I was then the chair of the Disability Ministries Committee of The United Methodist Church, and all I said then was a few words about what the committee did. God is so good! I am still stunned by what has happened because of that "chance" meeting and by the plans for the future that have grown out of this second disability consultation.

Interlude

Serendipity

Meeting by "accident"
Sharing my heart
Dream becoming reality
Seed becoming a tree
Shelter for those left out in the elements
Setting fruit to feed spirits
The fragrance overwhelms me
It is God's great goodness
I am on my knees in gratitude

7

Deepening Understanding, Finding Joy

Deaconess Chita Framo, "Retired"

Walking among people living in extreme poverty made my heart hurt. In Bocobo, a neighborhood in Metro Manila, people live almost on top of each other in very small homes built or repaired with scavenged metal and wood. There is no space between or in front of them. They wash their clothes in the gutter, right outside their door, using rainwater, which gets dirtier as it passes by each house. Everybody of every age is very thin. The smell of sewage made my stomach clench at times. Deaconess Chita Framo guided me through, talking to me softly as we made our way around the block until we got to the house and the little preschool next door, both owned by the Deaconess/Home Missioner Order.

Inside the house, Chita and I made and ate a simple lunch of vegetables and rice. I ate slowly, thinking about those living around us who do not have enough to eat. Chita explained the history of the house and how deaconesses who work at the school and in the neighborhood have lived there for many years. There has been a succession of women called to alleviate the effects of poverty in that place.

After lunch, we went next door to the preschool, which consisted of one classroom. It was open and airy and painted in bright cheerful colors that made me smile. Class was over for the day, but I could imagine the children I had seen playing in the street being in this room, singing and learning together under the guidance of their deaconess teacher. There, Chita showed me the hope found in the presence of the school by telling me stories of the children, past and present, who had benefited from their time in that classroom. I could see the presence of Christ in Bocobo after all. And now, every time I see Chita again, my sight becomes clearer, because her own vision is so clear. She finds hope in every situation because she is following Christ everywhere she goes, and there is no place she can go that God's love does not reach.

Deaconess Chita Framo is still in ministry despite being officially retired for more than a decade. She continues to travel to Diakonia gatherings and other meetings, to advocate for causes that impact deaconess/home missioners, and much more. She is a gentle woman with beautiful gray hair and an easy smile who reaches out to me in what I am sure is the same way she reaches out to other deaconesses and everybody else, with kindness and love and a kind of feeling of a happy secret together, the secret of what it means to work for God. From Chita I have learned that the deaconess/home missioner commitment to a lifetime of love, justice, and service is just that, a lifetime commitment. We sat down together at a table in the chapel at Decker Home for Retired Deaconesses and had the unhurried conversation I had long wanted to have with her, to hear her stories and memories, as well as her thoughts about what the future of the Order of Deaconess/Home Missioner in the Philippines might be. It had been more than five years since I first met her, and I was grateful to have the chance to spend time with her.

There was still a lot I didn't know about Chita until this interview—for instance, that she has never been married. She had become a deaconess before marriage was allowed, and she stayed single after the rule was changed. She has sometimes been teased about having suitors, but she seems very happy that her life has turned out the way it has. She told me why she had become a deaconess. When she was young, a deaconess had lived in her family's home. This was customary. All deaconesses lived with a family then. Chita told me that she wondered about the woman, thinking "What kind of a woman is this? She smiles a lot and people love her! Then she sings. She plays the piano. She teaches us and she goes around the community. I saw that she's so loved by the people! What kind of woman is so loved by the community?" When Chita was old enough to go to college, she wanted to be a deaconess like that woman, so she went to Harris Memorial College and became one. And she smiles a lot and people love her, just like the deaconess who lived with her family when she was a child.

She loves being a deaconess, laughing as she says, "It doesn't matter where I was appointed, or the kind of people, or the work they expect me to do, but I know that I love to do it!" She answered the call of God when she was a teenager. A few decades later, she is still answering God's call. Still gentle and loving and smiling her kind smile, yet courageous in speaking truth to power. Generous in teaching me about what it's like to be a deaconess/home missioner in the Philippines and helping me see the similarities and differences from the United States branch of the order.

She told me that deaconesses have not always had the right to vote on church business. This was an unjust situation, that they had voice but not vote in matters that impacted them as church workers. Clergy could vote but not deaconesses, so she organized the deaconesses and they stood around the room holding placards that made their case to the attendees of the church conference. The voting members recognized that the cause was legitimate, and they voted to approve the right of deaconesses to vote. It took courage for her to organize that action. It took courage for her to work to secure pensions several years later as well. Somewhat ironically, in 2024 at General Conference there was a vote on a petition to approve the right to vote for retired deaconesses, a right long overdue, since retired clergy have always had the vote. This time, the vote fell short. Perhaps Chita should have helped us organize. After all, she had the courage to start the chain of events that brought us to this point. We will bring this up again at the next General Conference in 2028.

This interview was different from most. I was trying to digest everything I had heard from deaconess/home missioners as well as other people I had met, so I asked Chita very different questions from the others I had interviewed. She helped me reflect and understand the Filipino point of view. There are many differences between our countries, not just for deaconess/home missioners, but in the cultures, in the role of The United Methodist Church and other denominations in society, and in the roles of deaconess/home missioners in the church. Even though I have learned a lot about the Philippines, my American perspective still dominates my thoughts. This conversation with Chita was very helpful in nudging me away from that habit.

For instance, I had heard that some deaconesses were leaving the order because the public schools pay higher salaries. A few deaconesses had told me that sometimes they could not afford to buy food. Their stories always ended with someone bringing food to their doors as an example of God providing for their needs, but that does not keep a few deaconesses from finding better pay elsewhere. And this situation does not help with recruiting new deaconess/home missioners. I thought my Americanized solution was simple—raise the salaries. But things are different in the Philippines, Chita reminded me. And yes, I know how prevalent poverty is, but I still thought my simplistic answer would work. Chita's idea is more realistic—to recruit more intentionally. And I can see how stories like hers, focused on a deaconess always smiling, never complaining, much loved by the people in the community, would be a powerful recruiting tool. And other deaconess/home missioners told me that working for God has blessed them beyond measure. This sounds like a recruitment plan that no other job can match. It was beyond my still-capitalistic thinking to understand what the deaconess/home missioner calling is actually all about, but this journey of the heart has brought me closer.

We continued to talk, moving on to how the world continues to change and how young deaconess/home missioners are always on their phones. This technology has potential for communicating with young people in effective new ways. It is my observation that the young deaconess/home missioners already know of many ways to do that, and there are young deaconess/home missioners at UMC headquarters, district offices, and in churches. I am thinking of Deaconess Grace, whom I interviewed at the A Women Leadership Training in Santiago City, Isabela, and how she continued to connect with the young people in her area throughout the pandemic. It seems to me that it wouldn't take much for every deaconess to learn to use this technology for Bible studies, for classes on other topics such as spiritual gifts, and even for preaching, as well as being very intentional about recruitment.

Chita also told me how she had been elected as president of the World Diakonia, a story that demonstrated the way God has worked in her life, always drawing out her gifts of courage and leadership as she has continued to follow her calling. While we didn't come close to solving the problems of the world or the church, our time together was valuable and fruitful. I am grateful, not only because she helped me process several things I had heard and seen, but because she is a role model of how to stay active and effective in deaconess work as I get even older. I look forward to seeing Chita again on my next visit to the Philippines or if she comes to the United States. She always, as she did that day in Bocobo, helps me to find hope in every circumstance.

Zarla Raguindin

I have known since we met that Zarla Raguindin and I share a passion to help people with disabilities become full participants in church and society, but I didn't know what was behind her energy and drive, so when we sat down in the covered patio at Decker House for this interview on a typically warm November evening, I was excited that we finally had time to talk. I had so many questions!

She is the first active Filipina deaconess I ever met, so it seemed fitting to me that she would be the last one I was interviewing, a way of coming full circle. When we started our time together, I had no idea how perfect this ending of my journey of the heart would be.

We first met in May 2014 at United Methodist Women (now known as United Women in Faith) Assembly, a conference held every four years. Participants come from all over the world to worship, learn, and connect. It was my first time attending this large gathering. I was there to colead a training workshop on that year's "Disability and the Church" study because I was then the chair of the Disability Ministries Committee of The United Methodist Church. Zarla was there to attend the class because her master's degree is in special education, and she was interested to know how The United Methodist Church was moving toward full inclusion of people with disabilities. She was already teaching at Harris Memorial College, so she felt compelled to know more about ministries that include people with disabilities in order to share that information with deaconesses-in-training. Lynn Swedberg, consultant to the Disability Committee, who, like me, was not yet a deaconess, was teaching with me. We enjoyed getting to know Zarla after the class finished. Her intellect and passion were obvious. We did our best to answer her questions.

When I began traveling to the Philippines three years later, I made a point of reconnecting with her. Since then, she has earned her PhD at Shaanxi Normal University in Xi'an, China, on a full scholarship. She is now teaching at Far Eastern University in Manila and continuing to teach at Harris Memorial College. She enjoys doing research to develop effective teaching methods for students with disabilities. She is a proponent of and an expert in universal design, which is an approach to designing architecture and school curricula in ways that are usable by everyone, regardless of ability or limitation.

Dr. Zarla Raguindin speaking at the Disability/ Mental Health Consultation, 2023.

One way to understand it is to think about curb cuts. First developed to allow wheelchair users to get from a crosswalk to a sidewalk, they also benefit people who use bicycles, strollers, shopping carts, and wheeled luggage. In an educational context, it is a method for designing lessons that benefit all students. This means teaching in ways that are appropriate to different learning styles and using methods that capitalize on student strengths while taking a variety of student needs into consideration. Visual learners need more pictures, auditory learners need to hear the information, kinetic learners need hands-on learning, assessment of progress is done in ways that best allow students to show what they have learned, and more. Rather than segregating learners, the goal is to develop teaching strategies to reach every student. I am a retired special day class teacher, and not only has she reminded me of what I once knew, but I have also learned many new things from her presentations at the Disability Consultations.

When we sat down for our interview in November 2023, we had not spent time together since the first Disability Consultation in 2019, more than four years earlier. Because of our common passion for inclusion of people with disabilities, I had always felt that we must have a lot in common. As she spoke, I began to understand how true that is, but I also saw the ways that we are different. Her intelligence and compassion come together in dedication to God and the church in an incredibly powerful way that helps me see my own life in a new light.

My first question for her was "How did you get interested in Disability Ministries?" Her answer began, "While I was in preparation at Harris [Memorial College, pursuing a bachelor's degree in kindergarten education], we never talked about children with special needs. And when I was in my first years as a deaconess, I was teaching preschoolers. Slowly I'm seeing diversity among my learners." She wanted to know more about how to teach to those differences, so she enrolled at the University of the Philippines, Diliman, where she earned her master's degree in special education.

Later, she came to Manila. In addition to her assigned work as a deaconess, she volunteered to work with the children served by the Asuncion A. Perez Memorial Center, which is a relief and community development agency of The United Methodist Church in the Philippines. It was during this time that she put into practice what she had learned in grad school. Later, she wanted to know even more, and that spurred her decision to earn her PhD in education.

But these degrees were not education for the sake of education or for selfish purposes. Zarla has a guiding principle that she lives by, one that will not let go of me, challenging me. My breadth of commitment has been widened by her words. She puts it this way: "Getting deeper on . . . the reason why I really want to put my energy on this, on that. I think the reason for it all is that whatever I have received, the same offering I can give to the church." She does this by teaching all she has learned to others, not only to deaconesses in training at Harris Memorial College and to undergraduate and graduate students at Far Eastern University, but also to church leadership at the two Disability Consultations held so far and to those who will prepare the materials and curricula needed by the churches to teach Sunday school, Vacation Bible School, and Bible studies to all people with all types of diverse abilities. This generosity of increasing her own capabilities, her own capacity, as she follows her own interests is a model for listening to God's call and responding, an example for a valuable principle of discernment and increasing effectiveness while also increasing joy.

Currently, Zarla is serving as associate professor of the Philippine Normal University (PNU), teaching in the Faculty of Education and Information Science. She is among the faculty experts in the special needs and inclusive education area. PNU is the country's national center for teacher education. Zarla hopes to make an impact on the quality of education in the entire country by training in-service and pre-service teachers to develop inclusive classrooms so that education can truly be "education for all."

All this education combined with her goals struck me as being very demanding, very serious, so my next question for her was "What brings you joy?" She began by saying, "Doing something relevant, significant, meaningful, especially to other people." She went on from there, talking about teaching and research and how she "cannot say no to the church," no matter how busy she gets. She became more excited as she thought about the Disability Consultation of a few days before, saying, "This [*sic*] disability ministries that we are doing here, we are starting something, so it excites me. We don't know where it's leading us, or how long." This is one way that Zarla and I are alike. We are both excited by something new, something we haven't done before. It's an opportunity, an open door, and we are eager to see what will happen next. She added, "It's everybody working together, following the same path. That's joy for me."

She added that she also feels joy when her students or church members finally see the importance of inclusive ministry and then ask, "How should I do this?" She feels joy "when all the efforts that I do finally really contribute something to the growth of the church, and I really have an offering to the church." I can relate very well to that. Joy for both of us comes when we know our time and effort have made a difference.

This, I think, is the destination I needed to reach on my journey of the heart, with Zarla showing me where joy is found. She has shown me that pure-hearted commitment looks like gratitude, that service is giving your curiosity, your intellect, your skills, your abilities, and every part of you to the church and community, and that faith is trusting God to help you persevere through difficulties and hard times until you find yourself in a future filled with excitement where you can participate in building the kin-dom of God. I find joy in knowing I am not alone in this work. Zarla and many others are in it with me.

I am grateful to Zarla for helping me know all of this. She was very generous in sharing her time and insights. I am grateful that God has given her many gifts that she freely gives to others, including me.

Conclusion

I HAVE REACHED A waypoint in this journey of the heart. Many of my questions have been answered, some completely and others in part, because there will always be more to learn. My journey to greater understanding, compassion, and solidarity will continue as long as there is breath traveling into my lungs and out again.

From the first time I set foot on Philippine soil in 2017, my focus has always been on the people I was meeting and not on the fear I could have been feeling. From hearing the stories of political prisoners to playing with preschoolers at a school for indigenous children in the middle of a banana plantation, from getting stranded by a typhoon and very nearly by a pandemic, from traveling over mountains and across the agricultural areas, I have had many experiences that have helped me connect to the hearts of Filipino people and to the heart of God. I will always feel overwhelmed by knowing without any doubt that wherever I go, whatever I do, God goes before me. I am grateful beyond anything words can express. God is good, and even better than good.

I have learned about the Philippines, about the land, the culture, the injustices, the oppression, the warmth of the weather and the people's hearts, the richness of the land and the love I have received. I have heard answers to questions I was merely curious about as well as to questions I was desperate to ask. The concerns and challenges I faced before, during, and after the pandemic sparked those questions—about how to remain faithful in the face of adversity, where to find joy, how to persevere—which were answered during interviews and by seeing deaconess/home missioners in action. There were answers to questions I had not even articulated to myself, answers that led to a clearer understanding of God's calling for my life.

I used to think I had two distinct callings, that my calling to Disability Ministries was coming to an end after ten years, and that my new calling to connect with deaconess/home missioners in the Philippines was completely separate. I was wrong. God created me to advocate for justice against oppression and human rights violations in the Philippines in addition to working for disability justice and awareness in both countries. My disability work in the US has expanded to reach across the Pacific, and it has grown to include justice work on behalf of other marginalized and silenced people, those who are victims of systemic oppression, those on the short end of the powerless/powerful spectrum now in the US. It's all one calling. It is all about solidarity, about *kapwa* (shared identity), and about God's *loob* (God's will, or, more accurately, God's essence).

Those Filipino terms have a great importance in my thinking now. At the beginning of my travels, I knew that the culture of the Philippines was collective, that is, communal. When all people are recognized as God's people, the common ground of everybody becomes more recognizable. Solidarity begins with becoming an ally to the marginalized and grows from there to encompass the concept of *kapwa*. This is a communal way of thinking, of being, a way that is based on a belief of an inner self shared with the community, a way that acknowledges that we are all interconnected and interdependent. Around the world and across time, many cultures, including in Israel in the time of Jesus, have been communal. One way of expressing this is that we are all in this together, that "a rising tide lifts all boats."

God's *loob*, the essence of God, is love. Love is something God does, and love is what God is, the nature of God. All of us are called by God to love God and love neighbor. The more we love, the more we become like Christ, the more of God's *loob* arises within us. And it is interesting to learn that "God's will" is translated to

"God's *loob*," which leads to love as being the entirety of God's will. Early missionaries to the Philippines translated the Lord's Prayer into Tagalog as one step toward their goal of being culturally sensitive. The English translation reads as follows:

> Make Your Reign come home to us. Make Your whole, most authentic and relational Self be followed. Give us today rice to eat. Do not leave us so we are not overcome by temptation.[1]

This version begins by honoring the importance of place/home in the lives of the indigenous peoples. Rather than trying to understand a God in heaven, God comes to them where they are. "Most authentic and relational self" is God's *loob*, God's essence. Following God's most authentic, relational self is following the way of love. Rice is the staple in the Philippines, not bread. Praying to be given bread would be understood there as asking for something second-rate. And the last line makes a lot more sense to me than "lead us not into temptation." It reflects the dislike of being alone that is prominent in Filipino culture. Instead, knowing that God is with us protects us from being overcome by temptation as we are strengthened by God's love.

This wording of part of the prayer Jesus taught the disciples to pray is a valid translation, especially given the communal nature of the culture of ancient Israel as well as the Philippines. The words that so many in the US have memorized reflect our own culture, with our history of kings who ruled over us and our understanding of God as a king. This prayer reveals a more relational God for a more relational society, a gentler God who comes to their homes and stays with them, bringing rice and providing strength to resist temptation. God who is more friend and loving presence than king. God who shares an authentic self with us as God did by sending Jesus to live among us.

As a result of all I have learned from the deaconess/home missioners of the Philippines, I understand more about God's faithfulness and power, about seeing God going in front of me

1. de Mesa, "Inculturation," 17.

everywhere I go, how to stay strong in challenging times. I now know the value of connecting with other people who are church workers, who serve God. The sisterhood (or, rather, siblinghood) is an important part of how deaconess/home missioners can continue to serve God no matter how difficult things get. Connection and relationship can serve everybody, not just deaconess/home missioners. Not only clergy. All people. It's what we were created for. We are built to love God and neighbor. Love is a relationship. Not just something we say or a front we put on. Love is God's essence. We must absorb that and share it with others. We must act from a place of love because we are God's children. Not only that, but life is much easier and more fulfilling when we work together, pray together, laugh together. I see now how lonely I used to be, how much more open to others I have become, how being connected to others allows me to be myself much more than keeping to myself ever did. It seems like a paradox, but I now see the truth of it. I thank my friends in the Philippines for this gift.

Thank you for coming along on this journey of the heart. May you know, as I have learned, that God always goes before us, waiting for us, always ready to take care of us, to give us more than we deserve, and to overwhelm us with love.

Epilogue

After this book was written, Deaconess Norma Dollaga was given the 2024 World Methodist Peace Award for her work dedicated to establishing safe havens for the survivors of victims of extrajudicial killings. As a deaconess, she has spent four decades working for peace and justice. She was quoted by United Methodist News as saying:

> When the sun rises, every waking up leads me to renewed power and inspiration to carry on the tasks and mission entrusted. When the moon rises and concludes the night to rest my body from all that gives me reason to carry on, I am thankful that the day passed with meaningful endeavors. Love, in its nurturing and transformative power, sustains us in our journey.[1]

She added one more insight that brought back memories of the night in 2017 when I first began to understand the breadth of what resistance encompasses. She said, "Resistance is a gift." I am grateful to have seen this gift in her. *Maraming salamat*, Sis! *Maraming salamat sa Diyos*!

> (Please read the entire story as carried by UM News on April 22, 2024 at this link: "Filipino Deaconess Receives Peace Award" | https://www.umnews.org/en/news/filipino-deaconess-receives-peace-award)

1. Mangiduyos, "Filipino Deaconess Receives Peace Award."

APPENDIX I

Methodology and Glossary

THIS PROJECT IS A combination of ethnographical (observing, documenting, and analyzing the beliefs and customs of a culture)[1] and phenomenological (examining human experience by listening to the people involved)[2] methodologies, supplemented by written resources. The bulk of the research was obtained using informal, unstandardized interviews, defined as "a specific pattern of questions asked," and "the interviewer has the freedom to organize the interview in his/her own way and in the most appropriate situation."[3]

I interviewed twenty-eight deaconess/home missioners in various regions of the Philippines, including the Metro Manila area, Pampanga (north of Manila), Santiago City, Isabela (further north of Manila), and in Southeast Mindanao (Davao City and the Cotabato region). Interviewees were selected by staff in the United Methodist Board of Women's Work office, for the most part, based on a diversity of age, length of service, and place of service (church, school, conference office, nongovernmental agency, ecumenical work, etc.). A few interviews were specific requests because I was interested in a particular ministry or situation (e.g.,

1. Ariola, *Research and Statistics*, 59.
2. Ariola, *Research and Statistics*, 60.
3. Rivera and Rivera, *Practical Guide*, 71–72.

a student preparing to be a deaconess). The diversity reflects differences in culture, economic status, language, the challenges faced, and the personalities of the deaconess/home missioners. All of this has had an impact on this project.

I have been very careful not to invade anyone's privacy. I have made a sincere effort to ensure that the people I have written about are comfortable with the result, giving them the opportunity to redact or edit my writing. I have modified my words to make them anonymous or removed the words altogether when necessary.

In addition to being in covenant community with the people I have interviewed, my decisions about methodology are informed by my awareness of the lingering effects of colonialism. I am doing my best to set aside my privilege and give the interviewees the power that I might otherwise have in this situation. My goal is to spotlight their work and tell what I have learned, not to make myself look like any kind of a hero.

This is my own story. I do not presume to speak for others. I am using quotes from the interviews to illustrate what I have heard and what I thought about in the process of learning, but this is my own journey. What does it look like to love my neighbor, to work for justice, to serve those around me? What does it mean for God to answer prayer? How can I pray when life is overwhelming? Where is joy? What is my purpose? I have heard stories of the pandemic, of economic hardship, of doing work that they have not been trained to do. I have reflected on what all of this means to me, and my theology has shifted as a result of hearing how they pray, find joy, live out their callings, and by what I have experienced in the Philippines.

Because I have been transformed by all of this, I want to share all I have learned with others. My hope is that others will be transformed by reading it.

Because she had the initial idea for this project, I began interviews with Emma A. Cantor. I spoke with her during the pandemic lockdown via electronic means. I also used the outside sources listed in the bibliography.

I recorded the interviews using the voice memo app on my iPhone. I backed up the original recordings to ensure that I would not lose them if my phone went missing. I transcribed the interviews verbatim.

I wrote in mostly chronological order, with some exceptions. This reflects my own journey as I researched and wrote the book. I first wrote notes in a journal to capture the setting and other details, then added in information from interviews that I found significant. I focused on my own learning with a focus on what I wanted to share with others.

Glossary

Deaconess/Home Missioner: A lay (not ordained) religious order in The United Methodist Church whose members are consecrated to a lifetime of love, justice, and service. The titles "deaconess" and "home missioner" honor the history of mission-oriented laypeople since the end of the nineteenth century. It is sometimes said that a home missioner is the male equivalent of a deaconess, but there are some females who call themselves home missioners, preferring a more gender-neutral title. Others refer to themselves as "deaconess/home missioner." That is the term I use in this book, in an effort to be both inclusive and economical with words.

The Order of Deaconess/Home Missioner is "a covenant community that is rooted in scripture, informed by history, driven by mission, ecumenical in scope, and global in outreach."[4] Being part of a covenant community was what drew me in to the order. We pray for each other, celebrate together, and share a dedication to serve God and neighbor.

4. From The Order of Deaconess and Home Missioner web page: United Women in Faith, "Office of Deaconess."

We have four mandates which emulate the ministry of Christ:

- Alleviate suffering
- Eradicate causes of injustice and all that robs life of dignity and worth
- Facilitate the development of full human potential
- Share in the building of global community through the church universal[5]

Diakonia: The Greek word "*diakonia*" means "service among others." The DIAKONIA World Federation is an international and ecumenical community of deacons, deaconesses, diaconal ministers, and other church workers whose call is to "service, justice, compassion and peace for creation,"[6] whether ordained or lay. More generally, the word indicates a source that can help its members maintain hope and faithfulness through relationship with one another.

United Women in Faith: Formerly named United Methodist Women, and before that, Women's Society of Christian Service. In the Philippines, this last title is still used in some applications. Reaching back through history into the nineteenth century tells us there were additional names for women's groups from predecessor and related denominations. All were mission-oriented. Women were sent overseas as missionaries, teachers, and doctors to places where there were needs. United Women in Faith continues to deploy Regional Missionaries in the regions where they live. These regional missionaries serve the needs of women and children wherever they serve.

5. From The Order of Deaconess and Home Missioner web page: United Women in Faith, "Office of Deaconess."

6. Diakonia World Federation, "Who We Are."

APPENDIX II

Devotions

Solidarity—A Devotion for the A ("Active") Women Conference

Jesus is talking to God about his followers (us):

> I'm no longer in the world, but they are in the world, even as I'm coming to you. Holy Father, watch over them in your name, the name you gave me, that they will be one just as we are one. (John 17:11)

I am here on my sixth trip to the Philippines because I am in solidarity with the people of the Philippines. What does it mean to be in solidarity? I believe it means to be in a mutually beneficial, equal-power relationship, in which each person supplements and complements the others, taking our place as members of the body of Christ.

Solidarity is relational, but it also embodies action. We don't *think* solidarity. We *live* solidarity! Solidarity means that I am with you. Even when I am not physically present, I am with you. I am on your side.

In the summers of 2017, 2018, and 2019, I came to the Philippines on Solidarity Missions hosted by NCCP (National Council of Churches Philippines). I learned a lot about being in solidarity. One of the most important lessons was taught to me by two men who had been political prisoners and had been tortured. I won't share with you the terrible details. When they were finished, I was deeply disturbed. Being an American—you know, we always want to fix things, to *do something*! So, I asked them, "What can I do to help?"

One of the men took a deep breath and seemed to be thinking hard. Finally, he looked at me and said, "It is enough that you are here."

I sat back in my chair, no longer ready to jump up and do something. He was talking about the ministry of presence, of just being with another person, without trying to fix anything. Solidarity is a ministry of presence. Right now, I am present with you in this room. When I am in the US, I am still with you in spirit. And it has occurred to me that the Holy Trinity is a solidarity. The Three-in-One is in solidarity within itself, among themselves.

In the passage for this morning, Jesus, talking to Creator God, says that he and the Creator are one. And he is asking God to keep his followers, asking "that they may be one, even as we are one." Speaking not only about the people back then, but about us, here, now, in this world. He wants us to be one.

Looking around at the world today, I see many times when we are not one.

We go beyond disagreement, at times, to fracture. There are disaffiliations from our denomination, which trouble us, disturb us. We pray for unity, but unity does not come.

Even more than disaffiliation, I see times when we don't trust each other, when we are less than loving toward each other, when maybe we gossip or judge or find fault with each other. When we fail to love our neighbors and maybe even ourselves. Where is our unity, the unity that Christ wanted for us? The kind of unity the Son has with the Creator?

Finally, I notice that Jesus does not name the Third Person of the Trinity here. Could that be a hint? Is the Holy Spirit our guide to unity? To solidarity? I say yes. Only by the power of the Holy Spirit are we in unity with each other. And not only by the Spirit's power, but because we share the same Spirit. I feel it here in this room, don't you? That Spirit that brings us all together, that comes out in prayer and praise. In joy and in ministry.

This is what we must share with the world, this way of finding our way past our differences to unity, past our hopelessness to a hopeful future, past brokenness to collaboration, past sorrow to resurrection, past separation to solidarity.

What we do here is a start. The Holy Spirit can make us one with all the world, if we let ourselves be guided into that unity.

We are one in the Spirit . . .

May it be so. Amen.

The Man Living Among the Dead—A Devotion for United Methodist Headquarters Staff and for the Disability/Mental Health Consultation, November 2023

From Mark 5:1–20, The Gerasene Man

In this story of Jesus, I am struck especially by the man's reaction to Jesus getting out of the boat near the cemetery. He ran and knelt before him, begging him not to torture him.

Have you ever run to Jesus and knelt down before him? What did you ask of him? Plead with him for? Did you beg him not to torture you? Torture is not the first thing we think of Jesus doing to us, is it?

But for some people—people who are tortured deep inside, by mental illnesses—it can be. After all, they are tortured mentally by their illness already. Why would Jesus change that? Why would Jesus accept someone with an unclean spirit? Maybe torture is the only thing the man thought he deserved.

In a society that believed, and even today sometimes we still believe, deep inside us, that mental illness is demon possession—that God sent the demons, sent the illness to us because we are sinners and we have failed to repent—it can still feel like God is torturing us—that God hates us for some reason that we cannot figure out.

Is it an unclean spirit that causes mental illness? Is it a legion of demons possessing us, with God allowing it to happen?

These days if someone showed the symptoms the Gerasene man had—the inability to live with other people, the howling, the cutting of his own arms—we would think he needed a psychiatrist, possibly hospitalization and some strong medication. And all of that might very well be appropriate.

But Jesus didn't have access to those things. What did he do? He called that legion of demons to come out of the man and go into a herd of pigs to save the man. The unclean spirits were sent into animals that were considered by the Jewish people to be unclean. The pigs then died by suicide by running down a cliff into a lake and drowning.

Maybe the man had been close to dying by his own hand as well. Many people with mental illness are, after all. It seems to me that was what Jesus was doing—preventing the man's suicide. Soon the man was no longer naked and howling, living among the dead as one who wanted to be dead. Soon he was "clothed and in his right mind." Fully sane.

And he wanted to follow Jesus, but here, Jesus in his wisdom said no. Go back to your hometown, he said. Go and have a normal life again, with people who have known you a long time, who love you and care about you, people who will be overjoyed that you are well again.

And the man went, sharing the good news of Jesus Christ—witnessing to everyone who knew him that Jesus had saved him. What a great story! What a happy ending! The one who once lived among the dead in the cemetery came back to the land of the living.

So now I want to ask: How do we treat people with mental illness in our churches today? Do they become outcast? Do we send them away to live among the dead? Do we torture them by isolating them, not letting them belong to our congregations because we are afraid of them? Do we help them get the help they need?

This question is not an easy one, I know. We are not Jesus, able to cure people and send their mental illness into a bunch of animals and be gone. It's not so easy for us to transform a mentally ill person into someone "in their right mind."

And I know that getting professional help for people is not easy. Sometimes people don't want to go. And it's not cheap. Psychiatric care is not like taking someone to a clinic for an antibiotic. I know that.

But not all mental illnesses are severe, and not all tortured minds are dangerous. In fact, most people with mental illness are far more likely to be the victims of violence instead of being the ones committing violence against others. In our Scripture passage, remember, the man removed himself from other people. He was cutting himself, not hurting anyone else.

So stigma plays a part here. And so does fear. Somehow we need to decrease the stigma and the fear.

One in every four or five people struggle with mental illness each year. This means that people with mental illness are already in our congregations. In a congregation of fifty people, about ten to twelve people are affected. And mental illness is something that most people don't want to talk about, don't want to admit they have.

When the Gerasene man was living in town, the people had chained him up, tried to keep him from hurting anyone else or himself, but nothing they could do kept him from breaking free and running off to the cemetery. No one came to visit this man who howled and cut himself. What did he eat? Where did he sleep? Jesus, in compassion, knew the man needed him, so he went there. Went across the Sea of Galilee to find him, help him, heal him.

And we need to follow him there. There are too many people—young people, especially—dying by their own hands. Too many people taking others with them when they are determined not to live any more. We need to go where others do not go, to find the people who need to know they are loved and cared about—that they matter. We need to follow Jesus even to where the people are living among the dead, with mental illness getting in the way of the abundant life God wants us all to have. We might need training. We might need the courage that knowing what to do gives us.

But we need to follow him.

Let us pray:

Gracious and merciful God, we know that you are with us everywhere we are, even when we live with inner voices—inner demons—inner struggles—that only you know about. Even when we live with obvious mental illness. Even when we howl and hurt ourselves.

We are grateful that nothing can separate us from your love! Be with us as we follow your Son Jesus everywhere and anywhere your people need hope and healing and love and grace. Lead us, Lord. Make your way plain before us. May we be faithful to do all that you call us to do as we build your kin-dom, one person at a time.

In the name of the one we follow, your Son, Jesus Christ. Amen.

Bibliography

Apilado, Mariano C. *Revolutionary Spirituality: A Study of the Protestant Role in the American Colonial Rule of the Philippines, 1898—1928*. Quezon City, PH: New Day, 1999.

Ariola, Mariano M. *Research and Statistics with Thesis and Dissertation Writing*. Manila, PH: Unlimited Books Library Services and Publishing, 2014.

Asedillo, Rebecca C. "When Did We See You, Lord?" In *Rice in the Storm: Faith in Struggle in the Philippines*, edited by Rebecca C. Asedillo and B. David Williams, 135-48. New York: Friendship, 1989.

Association of Women in Theology. *Pinay Magnificat: Living Out Our Theology*. Quezon City, PH: National Council of Churches in the Philippines, 2017.

Balatan, Arestedes. "Reach the Frontliner Missionaries—United Methodist Mission Initiatives Asia Pacific—Featuring Emma Cantor." GUMC.tv, August 27, 2021, https://www.facebook.com/arestedes.balatan/posts/4581209825232059/.

Butler, Em. "Mindanao: The Land of Promise, Holding a Key to Environmental Defense Worldwide." Sierra Club Redwood Chapter, March 25, 2022. https://www.sierraclub.org/redwood/napa/blog/2022/03/mindanao-land-promise-holding-key-environmental-defense-worldwide-liyang.

Daguno-Bersamina, Kristine. ""Palace Explains 'State of Lawlessness.'" Philstar, September 3, 2016. https://www.philstar.com/headlines/2016/09/03/1620063/palace-explains-state-lawlessness.

de Mesa, José M. "Inculturation as Pilgrimage." In *Mission and Culture: The Louis J. Luzbetak Lectures*, edited by Stephen B. Bevans, 1–35. Maryknoll, NY: Orbis, 2012.

Diakonia World Federation. "Who We Are." https://diakonia-World.org/who-we-are-history/.

Enriquez, Virgilio G. *From Colonial to Liberation Psychology: The Philippine Experience*. International ed. Manila, PH: DeLaSalle University, 2004.

Harris Memorial College National Alumni Association. *Going Out and Giving Back: Stories of Deaconesses*. Taytay, RI: Harris Memorial College, 2017.

Human Rights Watch. "Philippines Events 2023." https://www.hrw.org/world-report/2024/country-chapters/philippines.

Maggay, Melba Padilla. *Transforming Society*. Eugene, OR: Wipf & Stock, 2010.

Mangiduyos, Gladys P. "Filipino Deaconess Receives Peace Award." UM News, April 22, 2024. https://www.umnews.org/en/news/filipino-deaconess-receives-peace-award.

Mariano, M. Ariola. *Research and Statistics with Thesis and Dissertation Writing*. Manila, PH: Unlimited Books Library Services and Publishing, 2014.

Marquez-Caramanzana, Darlene. "A Journey of Solidarity: Ruth and Naomi's Story, Part I." UM&Global (blog), September 14, 2023. http://www.umglobal.org/2023/09/darlene-marquez-caramanzana-journey-of.html.

———. "A Journey of Solidarity: Ruth and Naomi's Story, Part II." UM&Global (blog), September 21, 2023. http://www.umglobal.org/2023/09/darlene-marquez-caramanzana-journey2.html.

Maximiano M. Rivera Jr., and Roela Victoria Rivera. *Practical Guide to Thesis and Dissertation Writing*. Rev. ed. Quezon City, PH: KATHA, 2007.

National Council of Churches in the Philippines. "Church Leaders Appeal to President for Peace Talks on the 30th Anniversary of the Hague Joint Declaration, GRP-NDFP Peace Negotiations." September 1, 2022. https://nccphilippines.org/2022/09/01/church-leaders-appeal-to-president-for-peace-talks-on-the-30th-anniversary-of-the-hague-joint-declaration-which-framed-grp-ndfp-peace-negotiations/.

———. "Talk About Political Prisoners, Too." October 3, 2017. https://nccphilippines.org/2017/10/03/talk-about-political-prisoners-too/.

Rivera, Maximiano M. Jr., and Roela Victoria Rivera. *Practical Guide to Thesis and Dissertation Writing*. Rev. ed. Quezon City, PH: KATHA, 2007.

Sobrino, Jon, and Juan Hernández Pico. *Theology of Christian Solidarity*. Maryknoll, NY: Orbis, 1985.

Strobel, Leny Mendoza, ed. *Babaylan: Filipinos and the Call of the Indigenous*. Sunnyvale, CA: Center for Babaylan Studies, 2010.

———. *Coming Full Circle: The Process of Decolonization Among Post-1965 Filipino Americans*. Santa Rosa, CA: Center for Babaylan Studies, 2015.

United Church of Christ in the Philippines. "About Us." https://www.uccpchurch.com/about-us/.

The United Methodist Church. *The Book of Discipline of the United Methodist Church—2020/2024*. Nashville: The United Methodist Publishing House, 2024.

United Women of Faith. "Office of Deaconess & Home Missioner." https://uwfaith.org/what-we-do/deaconess-and-home-missioner/.

Valmidiano, Elsa. *We Are No Longer Babaylan*. Moorhead, MN: New Rivers, 2020.

Velunta, Revelation. *Reading the Parables of Jesus Inside a Jeepney*. Self-published, 2017.

World Council of Churches. "Statement on the Human Rights Situation in the Philippines." June 27, 2023. https://www.oikoumene.org/resources/documents/statement-on-the-human-rights-situation-in-the-philippines.

———. "WCC Statement Condemns Grave Human Rights Violations in the Philippines." June 27, 2023. https://www.oikoumene.org/news/wcc-statement-condemns-grave-human-rights-violations-in-the-philippines.

www.ingramcontent.com/pod-product-compliance
Lightning Source LLC
LaVergne TN
LVHW012333100826
845148LV00017B/2133
* 9 7 9 8 3 8 5 2 7 3 3 9 3 *